WITHDRAWN
From Bertrand Library

Women and Politics in the USSR

Women and Politics in the USSR
Consciousness Raising and Soviet Women's Groups

Genia K. Browning
*Lecturer, Department of Continuing Education
Thames Polytechnic*

WHEATSHEAF BOOKS · SUSSEX

ST. MARTIN'S PRESS · NEW YORK

First published in Great Britain in 1987 by
WHEATSHEAF BOOKS LTD
A MEMBER OF THE HARVESTER PRESS PUBLISHING GROUP
Publisher: John Spiers
16 Ship Street, Brighton, Sussex
and in the USA by
ST. MARTIN'S PRESS, INC
175 Fifth Avenue, New York, NY 10010

© Genia K. Browning, 1987

British Library Cataloguing in Publication Data

Browning, Genia K.
  Women and politics in the USSR:
  consciousness raising and Soviet women's
  groups.
  1. Women—Soviet Union—Social
  conditions
  I. Title
  305.4'2'0947   HQ1662

  ISBN 0-7450-0330-3 (Wheatsheaf)

Library of Congress Cataloging-in-Publication Data

Browning, Genia K.
  Women and politics in the USSR.

  Bibliography: p.
  Includes index.
  1. Women in politics—Soviet Union. 2. Women—
Soviet Union—Societies and clubs. 3. Soviet Union—
Politics and government—1917–   . I. Title.
HQ1236.5.S68B76   1987   320'.088042   87-9604
ISBN 0-312-00953-4

Typeset in 11 on 12 Times Roman by
Just Words Phototypesetters, Ellen Street, Portslade, Sussex
Printed and bound in Great Britain by
Biddles Ltd, Guildford and King's Lynn

All rights reserved

To my parents

Contents

Glossary

Introduction		1
1.	A Feminist Approach to Politics	6
	Consciousness Raising	8
	Political Participation and Power	12
	Methodology and Source Material	15
2.	Soviet Women in the Formal Political Institutions: The Communist Party	21
	The CPSU: Its Vanguard Role	22
	The *Nomenklatura* System	24
	Women in the CPSU	25
	Soviet Attitudes	35
3.	Informal Political Activity: The 'Social' Organisations	49
	The 'Social' Organisations	49
	The Zhensovety	52
4.	The Zhensovety: 'Independent' Organisations	65
	Zhensovety—Structure and Organisation	65
	The Zhensovety and 'Independence'	69
	Party Members in the Zhensovety	74
5.	The Zhensovety and the New Communist Woman	81
	Economic Activities	82
	Political Activity	87
	'Anti-religious' Activity	92

6. The Zhensovety: The Conflict Between
   Consciousness Raising and Traditional Gender Roles 96
      Socio-political Activity 96
      Cultural Activity 100
      Activity with Children 103
      The Zhensovety and Male Roles 106
      The Zhensovety and the Soviet Family 108
7. The Zhensovety: A Pressure Group for Women? 112
      The Zhensovety as a Pressure Group 112
      Zhensovety Activists and Consciousness 117

Conclusion 120
  The New Communist Woman 120
  Zhensovety Potential for a Female Self-identity 122
  The Zhensovety and Contradictions in Soviet Policy 125
  The Zhensovety: What They Tell Us About Women
    in Politics 126

Appendices
  1. i. Table 6: Female Candidate Members of the
      Central Committee, CPSU 1986 130
    ii. Table 7: Women Elected to Central Auditing
      Commission, 1986 131
  2. Correspondence from Soviet Women's Committee 132
  3. i. The Work for Oblast' and Local Zhensovety 135
    ii. Tasks for Local Zhensovety 137
  4. Table 8: The Location, Pattern of Growth and
    Extent of the Zhensovety, 1949-1981 139

Selected Bibliography 147
Index 173

Glossary

ACCTU	All Union Central Council of Trades Unions
agitprop	agitation and propaganda
ASSR	Autonomous Soviet Socialist Republic
kolkhoz	collective farm
kolkhoznik	collective farm worker
komsomol	youth organisation of the Communist Party
KPSS	Communist Party of the Soviet Union (CPSU)
krai	territory
Krest'yanka	The Peasant Woman, women's journal
obkom	party district committee
oblast'	district or province
politburo	political committee of the Central Committee CPSU
Rabotnitsa	The Working Woman, women's journal
raikom	regional or borough committee
raion	rural region or city borough
RSFSR	Russian Federative Socialist Republic (Russian Federation)
sovkhoz	state farm
TsK	Central Committee CPSU
zhenotdel	women's department of the Communist Party

Introduction

Throughout the world in all political systems women are markedly underrepresented in positions of political power, despite different legislation on sexual equality. The USSR was one of the first governments to write sexual equality into its constitution. Its government and Communist Party (CPSU) have claimed consistently that Soviet women have full political rights with men[1]. Yet in keeping with all other industrialised nations, the higher up the political power structure, the lower is the presence of women. We are all familiar with the rows of elderly male look-alikes. Indeed the election in 1986 of Alexandra Biryukova to the secretariat of the CPSU Central Committee, the first woman in twenty-five years, warranted attention by the international media. There are still no women in the highest political body, the politburo of the CPSU.

Since the 1970s, a growing body of academic work, both Soviet and Western, has referred to women in the USSR. Research by Western writers has revealed the sexual inequalities existent within Soviet society in general, and in political institutions in particular[2]. Feminist concepts have increasingly been applied to this analysis. It has been suggested that women's low political status is due both to their lack of women's consciousness raising (CR) groups, and to discriminatory practices by the CPSU (Jancar, 1978 pp.110,115). Further it has been intimated in the West that the situation of Soviet women is more likely to improve from the impact of the Western women's movement than from changes within Soviet society (Lapidus, 1978, p.346).

At the same time, Western writers have contributed to analysis of the Soviet political system by investigating participation patterns in the informal political arena of the USSR[3]. This research into the role of the local soviets and 'mass' organisations, the Soviet 'interest groups', presents an alternative to the closed model of Soviet society which arose from the totalitarian perspective. However, women's participation in their 'social' organisations has not been included as a subject of enquiry. Yet Soviet women participate extensively at local level, in the soviets, the trades unions, the commissions attached to both, and in other mass 'social' organisations. They also have their own 'women only' 'social' organisations, the *zhenskie sovety,* commonly known as the *zhensovety*[4]. These are referred to as 'spontaneous', 'independent' organisations in which women work on their own 'initiative' (correspondence, Soviet Women's Committee). It was these organisations to which Gorbachev referred in his speech at the 27th party congress (1986), as a means of helping women, 'Women's councils could help to resolve a wide range of social problems arising in the life of our country' (trans. *Soviet News,* 23 June 1986).

Previous Western work on Soviet women makes little more than passing reference to the zhensovety[5]. Writers have tended to dismiss them on the grounds that they lack the autonomy of the 'women only' groups of the Western women's movement, hence do not have the same potential for raising women's consciousness[6].

Soviet academic research during this same period, however, has been concerned with women's informal political participation, and in this context has included the zhensovety[7]. Soviet theory suggests that women's political consciousness, together with the skills required for formal political participation, will be developed by their involvement in the 'social' organisations, and particularly the zhensovety. Yet Soviet academics fail to address the question of why women do not participate in the leadership of the CPSU.

We use this Soviet material to bring together the two areas of Western work in order to examine why Soviet theory on women's political participation has failed in practice to produce female leaders. The zhensovety will be looked at in two respects: how their aim to raise women's political consciousness is manifest; and whether they have the potential to act as autonomous consciousness-raising groups for women.

The first chapter will introduce the perspective which underpins this work. In particular it will discuss the significance of consciousness raising and autonomy in the context of women's political activity, and compare these concepts with their Soviet counterparts. It will also refer to the methodology and sources used for this study. The second chapter, Soviet Women in the Formal Political Institutions, provides the data on Soviet women's participation in the formal political institutions, with special reference to women on the Central Committee of the CPSU. It discusses the failure of the *nomenklatura* system to implement the party's policy of sexual equality. It then reviews Soviet explanations for this situation. Chapter 3, Informal Political Activity: The 'Social' Organisations, introduces the 'social' organisations in general and the zhensovety in particular, in terms of the Soviet policy of 'differentiation'. It traces zhensovety origins to seek explanation for their characterisation as 'spontaneous', 'ad hoc' organisations. The following four chapters look in detail at the zhensovety. The first of these compares their structure and organisation with the 'ideal type' CR groups of the Western women's movement. It then investigates the relation of the zhensovety to the CPSU, paying special reference to their 'independence' in respect to women's autonomy. Chapter 5 discusses zhensovety aims to raise women's political consciousness through their economic and political activities. This is followed in Chapter 6 by an enquiry into the effect of zhensovety 'socio-political' activities on women's consciousness. This chapter also considers zhensovety work with children, their attention to male gender roles and to the family. Chapter 7 looks at the covert effect of the zhensovety on women's consciousness by considering the zhensovety as a pressure group and the attitudes of the activists themselves. The final chapter considers the implications of these findings for women's participation, and concludes with speculation on the political future of Soviet women.

This book has emerged thanks to the encouragement of Professor David Lane of Birmingham University and the untiring supervision both he and Dr. Miriam Glucksman of the South Bank Polytechnic gave to my PhD thesis out of which it arose. Welcome support and useful discussion was also provided by the Women and Eastern Europe Group and the South Bank Women's Research Group. I am particularly grateful to members of the Soviet Academy of Social Sciences in Moscow for access to unpublished dissertations, and for frank and open discussion on both Soviet women and Western feminism. Those I interviewed in Moscow must be thanked for their patience with my Russian and their sincerity in attempting to answer my questions. I am indebted to the many Soviet women whom I came to know and warmly appreciate during my visits to the USSR, especially to my friends Vera, Lena, Tanya and Helen, and to Tat'yana Mamonova for the discussions we had in London. A special thank you to my parents to whom I owe my interest in societies other than our own. Finally, thank you to Jamie, who has waited so patiently for 'Mummy's work to finish'.

NOTES

1. The Central Committee resolution 'On the 60th Anniversary of the Great October Revolution' (31 Jan. 1977), claimed that 'a tremendously important task, that of guaranteeing women real equality in life—has been carried out *in full* in our country' (my emphasis), *Soviet News* (No. 5870, London Press Dept., 15 Feb. 1977).
2. The main works referred to are: Lapidus, *Women In Soviet Society* (1978); Jancar, *Women Under Communism* (1978); Heitlinger, *Women and State Socialism*, (1979); Atkinson *et al.*, *Women in Russia* (1978).
3. Friedgut, *Political Participation in the USSR*, (1979); Hill, *Soviet Political Elites* (1977).
4. The 'zhenskie sovety' have been translated both as the 'women's soviets' (Stites, 1978, p.414) and as the 'women's councils' (Lapidus, 1978a, p.207). 'Zhensovety' is the abbreviated form commonly used in Soviet sources.
5. Most reference was found in Blekher (1979) who devotes over a page. Other sources were mainly limited to footnotes: Lapidus (1978), p.208; Stites (1978) pp.313-14; Hough in Atkinson *et al.*, (1978) p.362; Jancar (1978) pp.107-8 who refers to 'women's committees' seems to

be writing about the trades union 'Commissions for Work Amongst Women'.
6. Heitlinger (1979) p.64, for example, dismisses the possibility of autonomous organisation for Soviet women.
7. Tallya, *Deyatel'nost' KPSS po Povysheniyu Ideino-Politicheskovo Urovnya Sovetskikh Zhenshchin v Usloviyakh Stroitel'stva Kommunizma* (1971); Cheidene, *Deyatel'nost' KPSS po Povysheniyu Roli Zhenshchin v Upravlenii Obschenarodnym Gosudarstvom* (1980); Zhvirble, *Zhenshchiny v Sostave KPSS i ikh Uchastie vo Vnutripartiinoi Zhizni* (1980).

1 A Feminist Approach to Politics

During three years spent working and studying in Moscow, I came to have a deep respect for the Soviet women I met. They manage so many roles, not only their mother and worker roles, but are also active in voluntary social work, all in conditions that in so many ways do not favour women. We know they work longer hours than men, have less leisure time, and are generally in lower positions at work, on correspondingly lower pay. What is not so well documented is their sense of confidence. Confidence in their right to work, and a confidence about themselves as women. Soviet women have internalised their right to equality, albeit an equality far from being realised and a limited one in Western feminist terms. There is widespread acceptance among Soviet women that they have the right to the equality promised by official ideology. They also intend to keep the gains already made—such as the right to paid employment. At the same time, the lived reality of Soviet women serves to contradict much of the 'official' claims about women's lives. Some women therefore question the very desirability of sexual equality. The exiled *Maria* group of the Leningrad feminists express one form of this (Goricheva in *Women and Russia, First Feminist Samizdat* 1979, p.31). These contradictions are also increasingly identified in the Soviet media and acknowledged by Soviet policy makers[1].

We know that women participate extensively in the world of work. Over 90 per cent of women are either working or studying, with just 4 per cent being identified as full-time housewives (1979) (*Zhenshchiny i deti*, 1985 p.47). Pensioners account for 19.6 per cent (1979) *(ibid)*. Women actually constitute just over half of all employees, 51 per cent (1983) *(Zhenshchiny i deti,* 1985, p.51). However, their participation, though widespread throughout the branches of the economy, tends to predominate in certain areas. Thus 82 per cent of health workers (1983) including 68 per cent of the doctors (1984) *(ibid* p.64) are female, and 75 per cent of those employed in education (1983) *(ibid* p.51). Women are also 70 per cent of those employed as economists, and 36 per cent in the traditionally male preserve of engineering *(ibid* p.81). In the law, another male preserve, 37 per cent of judges are women (1983) *(ibid* p.27). They are also 46 per cent of workers on the collective farms (1981). These figures taken on their own are impressive but, as we well know, occupational status and pay are intervening factors. The average pay for men and women in 1983 was 175 roubles in agriculture and 204.5R in industry *(The USSR in Stats.* 1984, p.193). The average pay for education and health, two areas in which women predominate, fell well below this, despite recent rises. Education was 142R and Public Health which is grouped with physical culture and social services, was 132R *(ibid* p.195). We get a clearer picture still when looking at career advancement in these fields. Nine per cent of chief engineers and their assistants are female; and 11 per cent of the directors of industrial combines *(Zhenshchiny i deti* 1985, p.30). This will not surprise women in the West, who face worse discrimination in these areas. However, the pattern of male advance at the expense of women is clearly marked in education and health, in which women predominate. In education, for example, for the year 1984-5, of the 75 per cent of women working in education, they were actually directors of the schools as follows: elementary schools: 83 per cent; eight-year schools: 42 per cent; middle schools: 38 per cent. However, women can fulfil the role of assistant directors: 66 per cent in the eight-year schools and 71 per cent in the middle schools (Vestnik Statistiki No. 1, 1986, p.66).

This familiar pyramid pattern of women in hierarchies cannot be ascribed to lower educational qualifications. Over half the university students in the USSR are female—55 per cent *(Zhenshchiny i deti*, 1985, p.44). Even in the central

Asian republics women are well represented in higher education, the lowest being Tadzhikistan with 39 per cent *(ibid* p.41). In the Baltic republics, the female population in higher education reaches as high as 59 per cent.

This picture of Soviet women is one of major advance in some areas; we in the West have yet to catch up with them in higher education, whereas in other areas they have yet to realise the rights expressed by the very existence of the Western women's movement. They accordingly face greater discrimination where we have made some headway, such as in control of our own bodies. In the West we have the space to express our demands, although our mass movements lack the power of the policy-making bodies. In the USSR, the right to formal sexual equality is written into the Constitution, but we commonly presume that Soviet women lack their own movement or organisation to make demands on the Soviet system. What Soviet women do share with us, is their under-representation in political power.

CONSCIOUSNESS RAISING

Soviet authorities and Western feminists both suggest that the level of women's consciousness is an explanatory factor for low political participation. For many Western feminists,[2] the experience of the women's movement indicates that political consciousness is most likely to arise from the collective development of female awareness. During the 1960s and 1970s this awareness was engendered by consciousness-raising groups. The zhensovety, women-only groups with the aim to raise female political consciousness, became widespread throughout the USSR during the same period. Both feminists and the CPSU have interpreted 'political activity' to include areas traditionally associated with 'women's work'. The practice of both has led to greater participation by women, but neither approach has had an impact so far on the position of women in political power. We consider this phenomenon by looking at the 'women only' groups in the Soviet Union.

We argue that the inferior status of women in Soviet political institutions results from the underlying biologism of male-engendered policies for gender equality. By *biologism* we refer to a 'prejudice based on sex' (Chetwynd and Hartnett eds., 1978, p.2) which determines gender roles by biologically assigned characteristics. A feminist concept of sexism is pertinent to an understanding of how the subordination of women is maintained. By sexism we mean the ideology and cultural practice which links biological sex characteristics to a hierarchy of roles according to gender.

Sexist ideology has justified women's exclusion, but more invidiously, made this exclusion 'invisible' by ignoring it. As Sheila Rowbotham (1979, p.26) has so ably articulated, women's experience of subordination has been their exclusion from 'all generalising concepts and from the dominant definitions of culture', with the result that 'common sense' notions of 'natural' inferiority have been internalised by women themselves. The actual inferior position of women in political power structures, as in all social institutions, serves to reinforce as well as perpetuate this perceived inferiority. Sexism takes place both within the interpersonal relations within the family, and in society at a macro level. Its general nature is obfuscated by its existence in the intimate 'face to face' relations of 'oppressor and oppressed'. Oppression is internalised and perceived through male definitions of reality. The dichotomy practised between the private and public spheres of life serves to restrict analysis of intimate relations in public. Politics of the personal, including sexual politics are therefore omitted in any explicit form from political theory. This hidden nature of sexism results in its lack of recognition, as well as its pervasiveness. For this reason, it is important to uncover the political mechanisms that support its continued existence if we are to understand more fully the absence of women in political hierarchies.

Feminist and Soviet definitions of political consciousness and the way it is generated differ though in crucial respects. In the experience of the Western women's movement, independent space from men has enabled a sense of self to emerge, a collective consciousness of being female. Women come to appreciate that 'their personal problems are not individual or inevitable BUT are generalised, systemic, socially caused and common', and need to be solved via political action (quoted

Nancy McWilliam, in Jaquette ed., 1974, p.160).

Soviet ideology recognises the common and social causes of sexual inequality and differentiates women as a separate social category for political consciousness raising. Sexual discrimination is acknowledged to exist in the USSR, but is considered limited to individuals, and a hangover from the pre-revolutionary system. Women's own sense of inferiority is seen as a psychological problem inherited from the past. Political consciousness is similarly considered as developing initially from individual awareness of problems as socially caused. However, the all-important distinction from feminists is that for Soviet Marxists this initially takes place at the 'point of production'. Consciousness is perceived as relating to class structure, not the lived experience of gender. In the public world of work, trade union consciousness can develop to class consciousness and eventually to political consciousness and membership of a political party (Lenin, 1944 'What is to be done?'). Thus women's consciousness is raised by entering the public world of production. With female political equality consequent on the economic sphere, the central political process of who participates and how power is expressed is presented as secondary and marginal. By maintaining that class divisions are primary, the revolutionary eradication of those divisions is understood to remove the basis for conflict in the superstructure. Sexual divisions are defined as 'non-antagonistic' (Titarenko, 1971, p.179). As Valentina Nikolaeva-Tereshkova, cosmonaut and president of the Soviet Women's Committee has said, 'In conditions of socialism, there are not, and cannot be, any classes with a stake in the political and economic inequality of women' *(Pravda*, 4 March 1975). What is not acknowledged is the existence of social inequality arising from the present gender relations perpetuated by sexism. The effect of the intimate aspect of sexual oppression is denied. On the contrary, early attempts to explore this dimension, by for example Alexandra Kollontai, have been actively repressed[3].

Feminists have identified the political nature of personal relations, consolidated in the social phenomenon of the family. Thus 'Politics is about power, and as much about the power that men exercise over women as about the power of ministers over nations' (Oakley, 1981, p.310). Male power in the political institutions is a logical outcome of this personal power; the sexism of their power in the private sphere underpins that in the public sphere. Whilst the power within personal relations remains unrecognised and unchallenged, women face a major barrier to participation in the public world of politics (see Okin, 1980, Ch. 12).

Soviet theory, though, rejects the validity of sexual politics and the role of the family as a pertinent explanatory factor in female political participation. The institution of the family has itself been strengthened as 'the nucleus of Soviet society' (Sedugin, 1973, p.6). The manifestation of raised consciousness is inextricably linked with understanding and support of the political ideology and policy of the Communist Party. Political woman is epitomised in the image of the New Communist Woman. The New Soviet person, though, does not represent a radical new image for the new society, because it too has emerged from a predominantly male culture. As Ol'ga Tallya (1975, p.4), researcher of the zhensovety says, in qualifying her support for 'women only' groups—in the final analysis, 'there is no difference between general political work and the work amongst women. There is no special "women's view of the world" or of "women's morality" '[4].

The definition of the concept of equality has originated from within a male hegemony, and is therefore a 'myopic image' (Oakley, 1981, p.39)[5]. The theory of sexual equality on which Soviet policy is based also remains locked in its male construction. As Hilda Scott points out,

It is only recently that we have begun to draw conclusions for the fact that throughout recorded history societies' needs have been defined by men, Marx and Engels included . . . .. One of the needs which is now being dimly perceived, is for a stereoscopic vision of the future which will take this into account'. *(Women's Studies International Quarterly,* Vol. I, No. 2, 1978, p.198).

Because one of the effects of sexism has been to define women's experience by a male culture, women need an alternative culture based on the gender commonality of their lived experience to challenge this male hegemony. We would argue that autonomy is necessary to enable women to have the space to define their own agendas in those areas of their lives governed by gender. The presumption that women in the USSR do not have that space is perhaps premature without first investigating the women's-only organisations. In the women's movement the emergence of the women's groups arose out of the practice and experience of women themselves. We will therefore look at the origins of the zhensovety to see whether they arose from women's needs or from the policy of the predominantly male leadership.

It could be argued that there is no need for such autonomy if, as Soviet Marxist theory maintains, there is no socio-structural basis for sexual conflict within socialist society. We consider here however, that sexual conflict does have a relative autonomy from class conflict and therefore the overthrow of one does not necessarily remove the other. In that case, Marxist support for autonomous organisation to serve the interests of the subordinate class should be as relevant for a subordinate sex, and will therefore require its own revolution for radical transformation. We will argue further that without that recognition, a sexual dichotomy will continue. But this requires a paradigmatic shift in Soviet theory.

POLITICAL PARTICIPATION AND POWER

Consciousness raising and the role of autonomy in that process thus differs for Western feminism and Soviet Marxism. Apparent similarities are, however, to be found in attitudes to the socio-political activities of 'low' politics[6]. Both Soviet political theorists and many Western feminists consider that women's activity in the community should be awarded the status of political activity. In the USSR the status of community activity as political has been institutionalised. Since 1976, for example, the local soviets have organised statutory standing commissions 'For the Problems of Labour and Everyday Life of Women and Mother and Child Protection'. Women's activity in the social organisations, such as setting up creches and kindergartens, is also defined as political. It is this informal and 'low'-level formal political activity which Soviet theorists propound as an avenue for raising political consciousness: Social work raises women's interests in collective, regional and state affairs. (Tallya, 1975) Alexandra Biryukova (1985, p.309) records that during the last two decades over ten million women have had experience of 'statesmanship' by their participation in community affairs through election to local soviets. Their membership of various commissions and parents' committees means they 'participate in the formulation and realisation of political decisions'.

Feminists have extended this notion to all areas of women's lives with 'the personal is political'[7]. This concept has enabled women to perceive themselves as political, and helped change the definition of what politics is about. At the same time, a critique of political power and the masculinism and vanguardism of the revolutionary party has been developed. Women's full participation in 'high' and formal politics, in addition to recognition of the value of community politics, is an issue of democracy. What Shelia Rowbotham (1979, p.59) refers to as a 'pyramid of levels of activity' which puts community and informal politics below that of the class struggle, can be seen as a denial of democratic participation for women. The lack of women in positions of power, and of networks for their representation as women, means that the male dominated political leaderships execute power at the expense of women[8]. The emergence of Raissa Gorbacheva as a visible wife of the General Secretary of the CPSU does not change the exclusion of women from political power. Indeed, suggestions that it does, demean women. It accepts that the way women can make their mark is through personal association with men in power, echoing what has long been the situation in the West. At most, the role performed by Raissa Gorbacheva, and media attention awarded it, can help awareness of women's invisibility on the political scene.

The omission of women seriously affects their ability to challenge the subordination of women in all its manifestations. Denial of women's place is a denial of the development of democracy. In modern 'democractic' societies, formal institutions are necessarily representative, with a complex system of interest groups supplementing the franchise. Increasingly, women have a political identity. The experience of women in the USSR has shown that much can be achieved on their behalf within paternalistic structures. But measures remain locked within the male paradigm. To democratise hierarchal structures of power, women have themselves to participate rather than rely on their representation by men. One woman in a post of responsibility does not significantly change women's representation. For a female input into the theories and policies governing Soviet society, women must have the real possibility of access to positions of power in an environment that supports a developing collective female consciousness of their general societal position. For women who do make the grade, the support and re-enactment of that awareness is a necessarily continuing process, if individual women are to avoid being incorporated into male political paradigms. To avoid the dangers of incorporation, women need to enter the structures in sufficient numbers and with support and accountability from women outside[9]. At the same time, it is vital for women to enter positions of political power, even when these are overwhelmingly male-dominated, in order to change the very nature of the power that precludes women. Indeed, sole concentration on informal political activity does not in itself raise women's issues to the status still accorded to formal political agendas, but can contribute to their marginalisation, for it leaves male power in control. As Marcia Lee (1976, p.314) has put it, 'Most women are restricted from holding public office because of their sex role assignments, and it is precisely because of their sex role assignments that women need to hold public office'.

Feminists and Soviet theorists, then, accept that activity in the community on issues emanating from female gender roles is political. Whilst Soviet theorists consider that women's interests are adequately represented within the hierarchies by male politicians, feminists are under no such delusion. However, rejection of the male bastions of 'high' politics contributes to the invisibility of women's non-participation. Feminist analysis of sexual politics quite rightly points to the need for women to distance themselves from men in order to define their needs. But implementation of these needs will remain problematic with women having no access to the political institutions which have the power to structure our lives (see Stacey and Price, 1981, p.189).

As we will illustrate by women's position in Soviet politics, without women themselves participating in the hierarchy as a distinct social category, their needs and interests will remain unrecognised and unfulfilled. (Walum, 1976, p.206). Women are well represented in low politics, and fully participate in community politics. But the barrier of the traditional gender-based dichotomy between private and public activity has merely been transferred to a sexual division of political labour in the public sphere between high and low politics[10]. In other words, we propose that without women in positions of political leadership within the hierarchies, any political agendas that women succeed in presenting will be masculinised at the level of power, and all other forms of women's political participation will remain subordinate. For a re-definition of women's politics and a re-evaluation of women's issues, women must be in the positions of power where that takes place. At the same time they need to maintain an interacting relationship with women outside the power structure. This study aims to show that the inequality in the Soviet political system arises from the sexism practised both within the formal and informal spheres of political activity.

METHODOLOGY AND SOURCE MATERIAL

We maintain then that women as an analytical category are crucial to understanding social systems[11]. Soviet reference to women as a specific category has had a descriptive rather than an analytical function as is most apparent in the context of political power. As in all comparative study, there is the problem of using perspectives and concepts which are culturally specific. Applying the experiences of the Western women's movement, in particular its concepts of autonomy and consciousness raising, to Soviet women with their differing culture, political system and ideology, faces this problem[12]. In particular, the ideology of the CPSU has meaning for Soviet citizens, and the extent to which it does should not be underestimated. The study therefore uses two criteria for assessing the zhensovety: their success in Soviet terms, and their potential in terms of Western feminist consciousness-raising groups.

In feminist theory, the importance of how the personal becomes socially generalised, and its effect on female participation, means that personal experience becomes an authentic focus for analysis. However, this authentic experience is partially mediated by the prevailing official ideology and its male hegemony. For this reason, analysis of women's position in a social system requires reference to the prevailing ideology. Thus areas of contradictions can be expected to arise from the synthesis of the female experience, and its influence by the official ideology[13].

Cross-cultural studies of the USSR, owing to problems of access, rely more readily on secondary and quantifiable data, rather than on qualitative research. As Zhvirble (1980) notes, statistical material on women is severely limited. This is further complicated by the pervasiveness of the 'official' ideology, which leads to a tendency for respondents to air an 'official' view whatever research techniques are employed. Whilst this presents a major problem, it is not insurmountable. Indeed, analysis of Soviet women serves to modify Bialer's description of a 'single culture'. The scarcity of references to women in party publications serves to underline their low position in the CPSU. Thus for example, in a collection of documents on party organisation, only one includes a reference to women, whereas a number refer to youth (Vetrov, 1973). The paragraph allotted women is frequently adjacent to one on youth[14]. The dissertations which emerged since the 1970s provide the most detailed source of information. The 'avtoreferat' [abstracts] are available in libraries such as the Biblioteka Lenina and Social Science in Moscow. Complete dissertations were made available by the Moscow Academy of Social Sciences. Much of this material also appears in book and pamphlet form[15]. Ol'ga Tallya in particular, whose research is based on her experience as Assistant Chair of the Chuvash republic Zhensovet, awards serious attention to the zhensovety.

The interviews referred to were held in Moscow (1981), with a member of the *Rabotnitsa* staff; with Tat'yana Sidirova, research specialist on 'women's affairs'; and with 'Olya', the Chair of a women's Trades Union Commission for Work Amongst Women. The interview with Sidirova developed into a lively discussion on gender roles with two other Soviet women who had come as 'observers'. As it was not possible to observe a zhensovety[16], the interview with the Chair of the trades union commission was most helpful. Although the commissions differ in certain respects from the zhensovety, much of their work overlaps. Attitudinal differences to the zhensovety were evident in these interviews. Correspondence with the Soviet Women's Committee (one letter of which is included as an appendix), was followed by discussion in Moscow. Conversations with Moscow acquaintances, both about attitudes to women's participation in general and to the zhensovety in particular, are also referred to.

Whenever possible, use is made of the first-hand accounts of zhensovety activists, their written records, and verbatim reports of their speeches to the women's congresses[17], conferences and seminars[18], and letters to the women's press. The written accounts have been produced as pamphlets, generally with a circulation of around 3,000, and in collections of material on the zhensovety mainly dating from 1958 to 1962. It was the extent of material published during these years which governed the selection of party sources. The early reports in particular are marked by their enthusiasm, and individuality in style (see Koval', 1961). These collections usually cover a particular locality and include contributions from party officials as well as zhensovety activists[19]. A. S. Stoyankina (1962) provides a most useful overall assessment of the zhensovety in the RSFSR [Russian Federation].

Party publications[20] and general literature on women make little reference to the zhensovety, apart from discussions on party policy in the 1960s and articles in the women's journals, *Rabotnitsa* and *Krest'yanka*. Other references provide little detail. This is likewise true of the press referred to in selected republics, during the 1960s and 1980[21]. The statistical data on the zhensovety included as an appendix have been culled from the various sources, as no collected statistical information is available[22].

NOTES

1. There has been considerable discussion on 'the woman question' in the Soviet press over the last three decades. For a flavour of popular attitudes to women, sex and gender see for example, *Literaturnaya Gazetta* No. 1 (Jan. 1979), and a series of articles and letters in *Komsomolskaya Pravda*. The latter are translated in *CDSP* [Current Digest of the Soviet Press] Vol. XXX, No. 42, pp.6-8. A number of Soviet films have also dealt with these themes, as for example, 'Neskol'ko Intervyu po Litscheny Voprosam' Gruzia Film Studio (1979) and 'Odnazhdi Dvadtsat' Let Spustya', see *CDSP,* Vol. XXXIII, No. 5, p.11.
2. Feminism defies a single definition. During its relatively short history, feminism has been perceived in varying ways, according to historical, geographical and ideological locations. As with other 'isms' perception varies both amongst feminists and non-feminists. The position taken here considers that recognition of women as a distinctive social group is an analytical category which has to be accounted for, and is as relevant a form of stratification as are class divisions for social analysis. The Status of feminism suffers from being perceived as the ideology of a subordinate group and is thus excluded from the paradigmatic norms of epistemology. This however does not invalidate it as a relevant theoretical tool.
3. Alexandra Kollantai's writings on sexuality were available in public libraries for a short time in the Khrushchev period, but were later withdrawn. Tat'yana Mamonova, 'Leningrad feminist', an editor of *Woman and Russia, First Feminist Samizdat* (1979), considered that access to these writings was a contributory factor in her own development as a feminist (conversation, 1981). Sexual politics is currently rejected as a 'bourgeois deviation' from class politics. See T. V. Kalinina, 'Kritika burzhaznikh fal'sifikatsii opyta resheniya zhensokovo voprosa v SSSR' in Esieva and Shilova eds. (1980), pp.72-4.
4. Legislation introduced on 25 April 1978 illustrates this point. It excluded women from a range of 'heavy' and 'dangerous' occupations and working conditions on the basis of predominantly male appraisal of women's abilities and needs as governed by biological characteristics. There is a significant body of Soviet research testifying to gender differences as evidence of sexual distinction. Research at Leningrad University, for example, claimed that analysis of 600 children's drawings showed gender distinction. Seventy per cent of the 6-7 year-old boys depicted industrial scenes compared to 6 per cent of the girls' drawings. Girls drew mainly houses, trees, flowers and human figures (quoted by I. Kon, 1975, p.659).
5. This is the dominant paradigm, however we maintain that change is endemic to human society. The ongoing process means that the ideology of sexual equality operates at a variety of levels, producing apparently contradictory attitudes. In this context it is interesting to

note that public discussion of the new Soviet Constitution led to a change in the formulation from 'women in the USSR have equal rights with men' in the draft to 'women and men have equal rights'. According to sociologist and journalist Ada Baskina (1979, p.10) this change recognised that the original wording had 'presented the rights of men as a model for women'.
6. Use is made of Seweryn Bialer's distinction between 'high' and 'low' politics. 'High' politics being the principal political issues of society, the abstract ideas, the language of politics, decisions and actions of leadership. 'Low' politics 'constitute the very substance of the Soviet system of political participation' (Bialer, 1980, p.166).
7. Feminists have themselves discussed the limitations of this concept. See for example, Tricia Davis, 'Stand by Your Men? Feminism and Socialism in the Eighties' in Bridges and Brunt eds. (1981), p.26, who suggests 'The personal is only fully political when it is deprivatized'.
8. 'The power of the powerful, rests after all on the powerlessness of the powerless'. (Rendel, 1981, p.15).
9. See Stacey and Price (1981), p.189, and Michele Barrett (1980), p.242, who refer to the need for a distinction to be made between more women holding political power and using such power for feminist ends.
10. Jean Bethke Elshtain (1974), argues that this dichotomy can be traced back to Aristotelian politics, and that despite female suffrage, the failure to challenge this bifurcation has meant that female participation remains limited.
11. As discussed by Gail Lapidus (1978), p.14, reference to women as a single category is itself a problem in that it subsumes socio-economic differences amongst women, but this does not disqualify the use of the category in this context. Whilst nationality does affect female access to position in the republic (Mickiewicz, 1977), the marked lack of participation by women in political hierarchies makes the generality of gender division relevant.
12. Hough in 'Women and Women's Issues in Soviet Policy Debates', in Atkinson *et al.* (1978), p.355, warns that there is a temptation to 'treat the absence of a strong feminist movement in the Soviet Union as a manifestation of backwardness of Soviet women's "consciousness" . . .'. 'But such an attempt would be of dubious methodological soundness, implying as it would be that the current feminist consciousness is the only "true" one'.
13. Bialer (1980, p.192), refers to the 'official culture' as the 'single culture' of the 'elite and citizens'. Whilst this provides an important alternative perspective to that of a closed elite imposing an alien ideology on an unwilling populace (see Conquest, 1967), it should not obscure an awareness that counter cultures also exist.
14. This pattern continues: see *Spravochnik sekretariya pervichnoi partiinoi organizatsii* (1980) pp.200-1 where women again follow youth.
15. A publication for example, edited by F. B. Esieva and G. F. Shilova

(1980) consists of five contributions based on dissertations: V. A. Zhuravleva, 'Deyatel'nost' partiinykh organiszatsii po pod'emyu trudovoi aktivnosti zhenshchin'; V. I. Cheidene, 'Povyshenie roli zhenshchin v rabote sovetov narodnykh deputatov'; N. P. Otke, 'Opyt raboty partiinykh organizatsii po povysheniyu obshche/ obrazovatel'novo i kul'turno-teknicheskovo urovnya zhenshchin (Na primere Kushkovskov khimcheskovo zavoda)'; S. Ya Zhvirble, 'Zhenshchin v sostave KPSS i ikh avangardnaya rol' v trudovom kollektive'; T. V. Kalinina, 'Kritika burzhuaznykh fal'sifikatsii optya resheniya zhenskovo voprosa v SSSR'.

16. Agreement to visit a zhensovet in Kalinin made during a preparatory visit was subsequently withdrawn.
17. These included material from the Uzbek and Buryat women's congresses, *s'ezd Zhenshchin Uzbekistana 1i, Stenograficheski otchet* (1959); *S'ezd Zhenshchin Buryatskoi ASSR 1i, Materialy s'ezda* (1961). The 8th Daghestan Women's Congress was produced as a booklet and included pictures and poems, *Khozyaika Strany Gor. Materialy raboty 8ovo s'ezda Zhenshchin Dagestana* (1961).
18. A report on the 3rd Moldavian Women's Congress, 'Bol'shaya Obshchestvennaya Sila', appears in *Krest'yanka*, No. 10 (1978), pp.32-4.
19. For example, V. Vaganov a contributor to a collection of articles on the zhensovety in Chelyabinskaya district (Kuznetsova ed. 1961) was a member of the *agitprop* department of the Oktyabr'skii *raikom*, Chelyabinsk.
20. A handbook on the CPSU for example, which includes 'Socio-political organisations' under 'Social organisations', lists the Soviet Women's Committee but not the zhenskie sovety (Struker ed., 1973, p.168).
21. Papers were selected for republics known to have zhensovety for 7-9 March, the period covering International Women's Day when editorials and feature articles give coverage to women. *Sovetskaya Latviya; Sovetskaya Litva; Sovetskaya Belorusskaya; Kazahkstanskaya Pravda; Sovetskaya Kirgiziya. Sovetskaya Litva* had two references to zhensovety (7 March 1980, p.1; 8 March 1980, p.2 and *Sovetskaya Kirgiziya* had one (8 March 1980, p.2).
22. Any reference to zhensovety in official Soviet statistics undifferentiates them from other 'social' organisations. See for example Belenkii and Rakhimov (1978), p.86, who use the records of the Krasnoyarskii Krai Soviet to show that of the 436,000 volunteers assisting the soviets in the area, 53,724 are members of parents' committees and zhensovety.

2 Soviet Women in the Formal Political Institutions: The Communist Party

Whilst politics is not reducible to the formal institutions, leadership positions within them play a crucial role in defining women's status. The more power a political body enjoys however, the less likely the participation of women (Haavio-Mannila, 1978, p.7). This is such a truism that the extent of female participation can be used as an indicator of the status of a political institution. This is as pertinent to the USSR as elsewhere. Sex therefore becomes a relevant category for understanding the political system (Harasymiw in Yedlin ed., 1980, p.168). As the USSR is a one-party state, the positions of leadership in that party are of prime significance. In most major respects, the participation patterns of women in the Communist Party of the Soviet Union (CPSU) echo those of women in the formal political institutions of other industrial societies. The Central Committee hovers around 4 per cent (4.63 per cent in 1986), similar to the governments of the UK and USA. The USSR has the distinction of having political equality of the sexes written into its constitution, but not only is this not reflected in actual posts, it allows official responsibility for low representation to be denied. Instead the onus is put on women. The aim of this chapter is to show that institutionalised sexism, however, is an explanatory factor. Female representation therefore will be examined here in terms of the extent to which advance is controlled by the party rather than by the wishes of women themselves. We challenge Soviet responses to the data presented by reference to two features of the CPSU, its 'vanguard role' and *nomenklatura* (appointment system).

THE CPSU: ITS VANGUARD ROLE

There is much debate amongst scholars of Soviet society about the existence and nature of an elite[1]. Of relevance to us here is that the CPSU defines itself as the vanguard and leader of Soviet society in general and of all institutions in particular. It is this feature which, together with the *nomenklatura* system, we will consider as responsible for perpetuating women's subordinate position in the political hierarchy. The vanguard role is spelled out in the Soviet constitution as follows, 'The leading and guiding force of Soviet society and the nucleus of its political system, of all state organisations and public organisations, is the Communist Party of the Soviet Union' (Article 6, Efimov, 1979, p.2).

This places the party as the linch pin of the system (Hill & Frank, 1981, p.141). Both the elected government and the administration are presented with policies emanating from the party. Party political culture pervades Soviet society. And whilst the relationship of the CPSU to other Soviet institutions is another area of debate, the CPSU intends its ideology to be the 'guiding force' for the building of a communist society. Party members are described in the rules of the CPSU as 'the more advanced, more politically conscious section' of the population (Rules CPSU, 1977).

These characteristics affect women in two major respects, one overt, the other covert. The first, more tangible effect, concerns the loss of career prospects. Party membership is not only regarded as a reward, it is the precondition for much of the career advancement in non-party bodies (Lapidus, 1978, p.209). Women are just 27.4 per cent of the party membership *(CPSU in Figures,* APN, 7 June 1983). It also affects those institutions in which women have made real advances—the trade unions and the soviets.

Table 1: Women as Percentage of Soviet Deputies

Local	50.3% (1985)
Union republics	36% (1985)
Supreme Soviet	33% (1984)
Presidium	11% (1980)

Table 2: Women as Percentage in Trades Unions, 1985

Membership	55.0%
Local committees	66.4%
Central Council	35.8% (1982)

Sources: Biryukova, (1985), pp.309; 313; 315; *Vestnik Statistiki* (1980), p.70, *Zhenshchiny i deti*, (1985), p.25.

Their numerical equality at local level is not reflected in the top-level posts which require party recommendation. The second effect is more covert. Whatever mechanisms of mediation exist between the party and citizen, the leading role of the party is exercised legitimately. Hence all issues affecting women specifically are ultimately defined by the party, namely its male leadership. It is claimed that CPSU membership bequeathes status—'To be a party member is a great honour' (Tatarinova, 1968, p.45). To the extent that this is so, the low membership of women, their small presence on the Central Committee and its secretariat, and their total absence from the politburo, can yield a perception of women as citizens with lower status than men.

This will only serve to reinforce traditional perceptions of women's inferiority and their unsuitability for power politics. The lack of female models reinforces not only male attitudes to women, but women's own self-image. In this way the exclusion of women from the vanguard contributes to the inequality amongst women and men in the political sphere. Women therefore lose out twice over: (a) they are not seen to warrant the 'reward' of a party post and (b) this denies them the avenues of social mobility available to men, thus maintaining women's low status. If it could be argued that the party is aware of this effect on women, and in keeping with its policy of sexual equality is attempting to confront the problem, then explanations for the lack of women in positions of political power need not include institutionalised discrimination by the CPSU. But this is not the case. On the contrary, women's poor political image is perpetuated further by another institutionalised feature, the system of *nomenklatura*.

THE *NOMENKLATURA* SYSTEM

Political mobility is effectively controlled by the *nomenklatura*. This is the system by which party secretariats sanction appointments to all major positions, both inside and outside the CPSU, and which applies to party and non-party members alike[2]. The patterns of female participation on the Central Committee shows that women are not exempt from this system, as Mary McCauley (1977, p.276) points out, the system is most evident at the higher levels. The extent of this control over female participation is also evident in the membership patterns of women throughout the CPSU and the soviets, as can be seen in the election patterns of female deputies. The proportion of women in the soviets has not only advanced steadily, but with a uniformity common to all regions whatever their socio-economic development. In 1975 for example, the percentage of women elected at local level ranged from 44.8 to 49.4, a difference of only 4.6 per cent. Similarly the percentage of deputies with party membership ranged between 40 per cent and 48 per cent (Lapidus, 1978, p.206). Within this pattern there are some regional differences, as research by Ellen Mickiewicz (1977) shows, and factors other than directives from higher bodies obviously account for these[3]. But the intent is one of planned advance. More importantly advance is restricted in terms of time and level. Zhvirble, who is emphatic that the increase in party membership of 1.3 million during the ten years 1967-77 was not spontaneous but consciously directed by the party, gives considerable space in her doctorate thesis to showing how those regions which fall behind the national average of female recruitment are urged to meet the norm. Following rebuke, female candidate membership in Kirghizia rose to 40.9 per cent, 9 per cent higher than the percentage of the USSR overall, and the percentage of full female membership rose by 4.6 per cent in just one year (19.7 per cent in 1976 to 24.3 per cent in 1977)[4]. Thus women can be found if sought. Such examples not only serve to show the extent to which women's advance is planned, but also undermine suggestions (Jancar, 1978, p.190) that one of the main factors in the low recruitment of women is the reluctance of women themselves.

It could be argued that planned intervention by the party represents a policy of positive discrimination rather than discrimination. Indeed, there is some evidence to support this view. Zhvirble (1980, pp.71-2) for instance, points out that 'after the 24th Congress, party growth was mainly achieved by youth and women at the expense of male workers', for her an indication of the party's 'constant care' for women. However, it will be noted that recruitment policies for women are in those occupations or regions where party influence is identified as weakest.

The intent therefore seems to be not to further women within the party in order to change the balance between the sexes, but to ensure that the party is represented, in accepted proportions, amongst all sections of the population. Whatever planning exists, and whatever progress women make, is ultimately controlled by the male 'gatekeepers' of the *nomenklatura*. It remains to be seen whether the appointment of Alexandra Biryukova, as a sole female voice on the highest secretariat, will herald change. A closer look at women in the CPSU will support the premiss that they are not encouraged to enter power and that women within the party career structure find their prospects limited.

WOMEN IN THE CPSU

In keeping with other political parties, the CPSU can be viewed as a pyramid, with its central bodies, notably the politburo and the secretariat of the Central Committee as the apex of political power. The base of the party are the primary party organisations (PPOs), to which every party member belongs. Members are elected to serve on committees at varying levels:*raikom* (borough or rural committee); *gorkom* (town), *obkom* (district and province) and *kraikom* (territory). Each level has its own bureau *(secretariat)*, of elected members who meet more frequently. In addition, there is an administration (the *apparat)* of full-time officials who implement decisions, and a range of specialist departments such as agitation and propaganda *(agitprop)*. Each republic, with the exception of the RSFSR, has its own Central Committee[5]. As can be seen from Table 3, female representation on committees is commensurate with female membership, with two exceptions. Women are over-represented at primary level, and under-represented on the All-union Central Committee. Women feature in particular as secretaries of the PPOs. These are mainly voluntary posts, only 5 per cent being full-time (Harasymiw in Yedlin ed. 1980, p.173) and require a considerable amount of 'social' work. They therefore 'fit' the traditional sphere of acceptable female public work.

Table 3: Women elected to party committees 1980-1 (1975-6)

	% of all elected	
Secretaries/members of work-place groups	22.9%	(20.6%)
Secretaries of primary organisations	35.1	(31.5)
Members of party committees of PPOs	27.9	(31.5)
Members and candidate members of district/raion and town organisations	31.2	(28.9)
Members and candidate members of provinces, union republic CCs and inspections committees	24.2	(22.9)

Source; CDSP, Vol. XXXIII, No. 38 (21 October 1981), p.1.

In some regions the over-representation of women in PPO posts is notably high. In Lithuania, Latvia (1977), between 40 and 49 per cent of secretaries were female (Zhvirble, 1980, p.143)[6]. But even in these regions, such over-representation does not extend to the higher levels. In Lithuania in 1973 for example, 36.7 per cent of PPO secretaries were female, but this fell to 18.2 per cent at *raikom* level and 13.9 per cent at *gorkom* level (Harasymiw, 1980, p.173). These are the figures for all secretaries. There is a sharp drop in the more important post of first secretary. Of the 18.2 per cent of female secretaries at *raikom* level, just 2.3 per cent of these were first secretaries. In reality it means that of the women prepared to be secretaries, only 2.3 per cent hold a post which could expect to lead to career advancement in the party *(ibid)*. Here the role of the *nomenklatura* is evident.

The limits of women's participation can be seen even more clearly in the types of post of responsibility that they hold. General statistics on participation do not in themselves provide adequate information about access to decision making. These must be qualified by the nature of the post, in particular its relation to the control of the political agenda and, in the Soviet case, to the *nomenklatura*. Women in all industrial societies have generally remained in 'the female ghetto', posts closely associated with female gender roles in the sexual division of labour. Women's public responsibilities thus echo their responsibilities in the private sphere. In this respect the USSR follows the general pattern of female participation. With few exceptions, women are found in health, social welfare, culture, education and youth. Women do not hold the key decision-making posts in the economy and home and foreign policy[7]. This limitation of women's participation is further underlined by their omission from all posts directly concerned with defence and foreign policy. Given the association of women with peace, which according to Soviet sources is the cornerstone of their foreign policy, their omission, as Jancar (1978, p.111) points out, is particularly marked.

The one area where women are well represented which does not arise directly from their traditional gender roles, is ideological work. Even here though, a connection can be detected. The high sense of duty which women are deemed to have is considered compatible with the 'moral codeks' of building communism which is emphasised in ideological work[8]. Around 50 per cent of the party's propaganda posts are filled by women[9]. In Moscow and Latvia female 'ideological organisers' reached as high as 70 per cent (1977-9) (Zhvirble, 1980, p.164). Much of this ideological activity is at local level[10]. As Moses (1978, pp.342-3) has shown it has low status and offers little career advancement. The relatively high representation of women thus presents no threat to male power.

Women and the Central Committee
It is evident then that women do feature at the lower levels of the party and whilst it is by no means on an equal basis to men, the situation is steadily improving. The present concern though is with the access of women to political power, so we now turn to the position of women on the All Union Central

Committee of the CPSU. In theory the Central Committee (CC), which is elected by the party congress, is the most authoritative committee in the party, acting as its ruling body between congresses. On it serve the party leaders, top government and state officials, representatives of 'social' organisations such as the trade unions, the Komsomol and the Women's Committee, leading figures from the arts and sciences, and honoured workers[11]. The committee consists of both full and candidate members, the latter without voting powers. Over time it has become a very large body, which meets only twice a year. At the 27th congress (1986) the number of full members was reduced for the first time since Stalin, from 319 (1981) to 307. However, the combined membership of full and candidate members increased. In practice it is actually the politburo, the smaller body elected by the Central Committee, which assumes policy and decision-making power. The other important body is the central secretariat which consists of top party secretaries and heads of the Central Committee departments. It provides information and policy recommendations for the politburo and Central Committee and governs cadres. The Central Auditing Commission (CAC), a 'junior member' of the hierarchy which audits party accounts, is also elected by congress.

Central Committee members represent those interest groups considered to be the most important in Soviet society. Hence the concern of Sovietologists to monitor change in the proportion of seats held by a particular bloc, such as the military. As an indicator of political importance, the size of the women's bloc is significant. The proportion of women is marked by its consistency. Since 1918, combined full and candidate members have only reached above 4 per cent a handful of times, 1918 (which in actual numbers represented only one woman); 1927; 1966; 1981 and 1986. The 27th congress percentage of 4.63 per cent has the distinction of being the highest ever achieved, both in percentage and absolute terms. It represents thirteen full members out of 307 and nine candidate members out of 168, a total of twenty-two in a body of 475. Given that the number of full members had remained constant at eight for the 25th and 26th congresses, their increase to thirteen marks a definite change. However this is hardly the 'feminisation' called for by Gorbachev. It makes no real inroads into changing women's position. This is further underlined by looking at the occupation and position of the female members. Seven of the eight women newly elected to full membership are 'worker' representatives, with only one of them (V. N. Pletneva) identified with responsibility at national level. This pattern is common in the female representation on the CC, as will be shown by more detailed reference to the 1981 membership.

At the 26th Party congress held in 1981, nineteen women were elected to the CC—eight full members, eleven candidate members. Their occupational patterns followed that of previous years. Ten women held 'official' positions, that is posts in the CPSU, the government, the state apparatus and 'social' organisations. The remaining nine were all workers from low-status occupations, with responsibilities such as brigade leader. This is particularly marked amongst the candidate members. Whereas six full members were officials, only three of the candidate members were, and one of these O. P. Kol'china had remained a candidate member for twenty years.

The posts are themselves of an inherited pattern as can be seen from Table 4. Between the 19th and 26th congresses, the only two women to have held posts above *oblast'* (district level, (O. Ivashchenko, secretary of the Ukraine CC and E. A. Furtseva, member of the politburo), did so under Khrushchev. Neither became a role model for other women to emulate. Until the appointment of Biryukova, the highest party post occupied by women on the CC was as second secretary on *oblast'* committees. Three women have held posts at this level: O. P. Kol'china, L. P. Lykova and Z. M. Kruglova[12]. Yet none of these women held the posts as full members of the CC. Kruglova became a full member in 1976 after holding the post of Chair of the Presidium of the Soviet Socialist Union of Friendship with Foreign Countries for two years. As a secretary of the Leningrad *obkom* she had been a member of the Auditing Committee. Lykova was a candidate member whilst a second secretary, but only became a full member as deputy Chair to the RSFSR Council of Ministers. Both these posts have had previous female representation on

Table 4: Career patterns of female members of the Central Committee (full and candidate) known to have held party position: 18-26th Congresses CPSU

Name	Date of birth	Date on CC	Post
Furtseva E. A.	(1910)	1952-71	1950-4 2nd sec. gorkom Moscow 1954-7 1st sec. gorkom Moscow 1956-60 sec. CC 1956-7 candid. presidium (politburo) 1957-61 full presidium
Ivashchenko O. I.	(1906)	1956 C 1961 F	1954-65 sec. CC Ukraine CP
Kol'china O. P.	(1918)	1961-81 C	1947-60 1st sec. gorkom – Krasnoiya Gorka 1960-3 2nd sec. obkom – Moscow 1964-7 sec. obkom – Moscow
Lykova L. P.	(1913)	1952-76 C	-1955 2nd sec. obkom Ivanovo 1958-61 2nd sec. obkom Smolensk
		1976-81 F	1961-7 RSFSR Ministry of Social Security
		-1981	Dep. chair RSFSR CoMinist. chair Anti-Alcoholism committee
Dement'eva R. F.	(1925)	1966-76 C 1976-81 F	1960-80 sec. Moscow gorkom 1981 2nd sec. Moscow gorkom
Kruglova A. M.	(1923)	1966-71 A	1963-8 sec. gorkom Leningrad 1968-74 sec. obkom Leningrad
		1976-81 F	1974 chair presidium USSR. Friendship & Cultural Relations with Foreign Countries 1974-5 USSR Dep. Min. of Culture
Andreevna N. A.		1956 C	1956 1st sec. raikom Bauman (M) 1960 Party control committee
Ivanova T. G.	(1940)	1981 C	1981 1st sec. raikom Kalinin (M)
Eliseeva N. G.	(1927)	1971 A 1976 F	1968-74 1st sec. raikom Nevsky (L) 1974.. Dep. chair Leningrad City Soviet exec. committee
Poberei M. T.		1966-76 C	1st sec. raikom Leninsk (Volgograd obl.)
Khmara I. G.	(1938)	1981 C	1981 1st sec. raikom Slagominska (Krasnodar krai)

Key
A auditing commission
C candidate member
F full member
M Moscow
L Leningrad

Sources:Pravda 4 March 1981. Herwig Kraus, *The Composition of the Leading Organs of the CPSU* (1951-82) (Munich, Radio Free Europe, 1982) pp.156-9.
Lapidus, *Women in Soviet Society* (1978) Table 27, p.218.
B. Lewytzkyi & J. Stroynowski eds. *Who's Who in the Socialist Countries* (New York, Saur, 1978).
M. McAndrew, 'The Extent of the Participation of Women in the Soviet Political System' (1977).

the CC. Kol'china remained a candidate member until the 27th congress, when she was dropped altogether.

Of these 1981 members, only three currently held posts within the party, the highest at *gorkom* (town) level. R. F. Dement'eva as second secretary of the Moscow *gorkom* had the distinction of being promoted (1980) after having been elected as a full CC member (1976). However, this proved to be short-lived: she was dropped at the following congress, in 1986. Two other members in 1981 held posts at *raion* (borough/rural) level, both candidate members elected in 1981. One of these I. G. Khmara was dropped in 1986, the other T. G. Ivanova remains a candidate member. They themselves had replaced a first secretary of the Leninsk *raikom* (Volgo oblast'). All other women to have held office at this level since the 19th congress did so as candidate members, and remained for only short periods. Khmara has been replaced in 1986 by Z. I. Borovikova, first secretary of Kurganinsk *raikom* as a candidate member. So the pattern continues.

Of the other members with 'official' positions in 1981, the cosmonaut Valentina Nikolaevna-Tereshkova is a member of the Supreme Soviet and Chair of the Soviet Women's Committee, one of the 'social' posts warranting representation on the CC. Alexandra Biryukova was secretary of the All Union Council of Trade Unions (AUCCTU) and E. F. Karpova and L. P. Lykova were both deputy Chairs of the RSFSR Council of Ministers. Whereas Karpova remained in 1986, Lykova was replaced—presumably by V. S. Shevchenko, who holds another government position, Chair of the presidium of the Ukranian Supreme Soviet.

Two general features of women's position emerge from this data. Firstly, the highest status within the party which women on the CC represent is limited to *obkom*. Posts above that do not warrant a place for women on the CC. Secondly, women who reach this level are then redirected into government or other non-party posts, all of which have less direct access to policy-making. This has been the case for a twenty-five year period, from Ekaterina Furtseva to Alexandra Biryukova.

The worker representatives on the 1981 CC likewise followed similar patterns to previous representation (see

Lapidus, 1978, p.230). Four have been identified as brigade and team leaders. Four were machine operators. Of the remaining two, one is an adjustor and the other a weaver. The common characteristic of these women is the contribution they make to production and their representation of those occupations in which women particularly feature. Their role appears to be what Lapidus has dubbed as 'the populist aura to the elite' *(ibid)*. Worker representatives do not serve for long terms on the CC. Of the candidate members elected in 1976 none remained for a second term of office.

A short profile of V. N. Golubeva will serve to illustrate the 'ideal type' of female worker awarded a place on the Central Committee. Valentina Golubeva (born 1947) is a weaver at the Ivanovskovo Kambol'novo Kombinat (Ivanovo, RSFSR). Her speech to the 26th congress indicates the reason for her election. The speech, which began by eulogising Brezhnev, focussed on her production achievements: 'I worked on more than a million metres of cloth and fulfilled in five years the task of 20 years. It is my worker's present to the 26th Congress of our Communist Party' (applause). She promises to increase her production still further and pass on her experience to young weavers *(Pravda,* 25 March, 1981, pp.4-5). In addition to this activity, a feature article on Golubeva presents her as an 'all-round' person: she studies part-time at a textile institute, is interested in nature and music, devoted to her family—a person who makes 'demands on herself'. The accompanying photo, of a smiling Valentina, leads to the comment, 'She really is often smiling—the broad smile of a happy person' (Skylar, *Rabotnitsa,* No. 11, 1981, p.2) (see also *Soviet Weekly,* 17 August, 1985, p.8). Tat'yana Sidirova also spoke of her as an interesting woman who she thought would 'rise fast'. 'She is so bright, with a comprehensive world outlook and versatile interests. A very remarkable person. You would think a mere weaver . . . but she soars. A brilliant speaker, grasps the point immediately'. Although apart from her obvious contribution as a worker, little was known of her political experience. Here we have then the complete prototype of the 'ideal type' New Communist Woman. Golubeva's election to the Central Committee provides a model for other working women to emulate.

Table 5: Female Members of the Central Committee CPSU 1986

Name	Date of Birth	Date CAC	Elected cand.	full	Post date	post
BIRYUKOVA Aleksandra Pavlovna	1929		1971	1976		Secretary, Presidium, All Union Council of Trade Unions; Secretariat, CC CPSU
CHERKASHINA Valentina Nikolaevna	1942	1976		1986	1986	Spinner, Volgograd *oblast'*, RSFSR
ERSHOVA Neli Mikhailovna	1939		1981	1986		Adjuster, machine building plant, RSFSR
GOLUBEVA Mariya Arkhipova	1945		1981	1986		Brigade leader, milking machine operator, *sovkhoz*, Biisk *raion*, Altai Krai, RSFSR
GOLUBEVA Valentina Nikolaevna	1949			1981		Weaver, Ivanovo worsted combine, Ivanovo *oblast'*, RSFSR
GROMOVA Mariya Sergeevna	1929	1981		1986		Milking machine operator, *sovkhoz*, Leninskii, *raion*, *Moscow oblast'*
KARPOVA Evdokiya Fedorovna	1923		1966	1976		Deputy Chair, Council of Ministers, USSR
KRUGLOVA Zinaida Mikhailovna	1923	1966		1976	1963-8 1968-74 1974	Secretary Leningrad *gorkom*; Secretary Leningrad *obkom*; Chair, Presidium, Union of Soviet Societies for Friendship & Cultural Relations with Foreign Countries; USSR Deputy Min. of Culture
NIKOLAEVA-TERESHKOVA Valentina Vladirmirovna	1937			1971	1974-5	Chair, Soviet Women's Committee; member of Presidium, USSR Supreme Soviet
PEREVERZEVA Nina Vasil'evna	1929		1981	1986		Team leader, *kolkhoz*, Peschanokorskoe *raion*, Rostov *oblast'*, RSFSR
PLETNEVA Valentina Nikolaevna	1930			1986		Weaver, Kostroma flax combine, RSFSR; member of Presidium, AUCCTU
SHEVCHENKO Valentina Semenovna	1935			1986		Chair, Presidium, Ukrainian SSR Supreme Soviet
UDALAYA Raisa Sitant'evna	1931	1981		1986		Riveter, Novosibirsk Aviation Plant, RSFSR

Sources: Pravda (4 March 1981; 7 March 1986); Belitsky *et al.* (1 April 1986); Herwig Krauss. (1982) *The Composition of the Leading Organs of the CPSU*, 1952-82 (Munich, Radio Free Europe); Cocks, Daniels and Heer eds. (1976) *The Dynamics of Soviet Politics* (Cambridge, Mass./London, Harvard University Press).

Whilst the occupational status of the 1981 CC differed little from previous terms, there was a marked difference with respect to age. Compared to 1976, the 1981 members were noticeably younger. Of the 1976 members, only one would have been under fifty years in 1981, whereas only one of the new members elected in 1981 was over fifty years. This suggests that a decision was made to elect younger women for the 26th congress. The 27th congress did not repeat this pattern, it did however consolidate the age group. The two oldest members (born 1913 and 1918) have been dropped. At thirty-seven years of age, Valentina Golubeva remains the youngest member.

Although the elections at the 27th party congress are interesting in that they increase female participation to its highest ever, and are marked by the promotion of a serving member of the CC to the secretariat, in most respects they follow the pattern of previous congresses (Table 5 full: see Appendix 1 for candidate and CAC female members). As mentioned earlier, the sizeable increase of full members from eight to thirteen is not as impressive as first appears. The seven new worker representatives follow the traditionally represented occupations: V. N. Cherkashina is a spinner; N. M. Ershova—adjustor; M. A. Golubeva—brigade leader, milk machine operator; M. S. Gromova—milk machine operator; N. V. Pereverzeva—team leader of a collective farm (kolkhoz); V. N. Pletneva—weaver, member of presidium of AUCCTU; R. S. Udalaya—riveter. Only one, V. S. Shevchenko, appears to be on the CC for her position in government, although it is probable that V. N. Pletneva has been elected as a member of the trade unions presidium rather than as a weaver. In other words the increase in female representation does not arise from amongst those women already in posts of responsibility and influence. The number of women in party and government posts remains the same as on the previous CC. The loss of R. F. Dement'eva, means that even with Biryukova's promotion there is no increase in women who hold party positions on the CC. This puts the election of Biryukova into context. No general advance has been made by women in the party.

As in previous elections, most of the full members had

either been candidate members or served on the CAC, three of the new members have been promoted from candidate membership and three from the CAC. It is therefore evident that both the CAC and candidate membership can be a form of training for full membership. Of the nine candidate members elected in 1986, all but two are new. Two of these are first secretaries at *raikom* level, bringing the total to three, the others are worker representatives, one of whom N. V. Gellert, has been identified as a deputy to the Supreme Soviet. Only two of the nine had had experience on the CAC. There are nineteen women on the 1986 CAC, all but three of whom have been identified as newly elected. A. L. Nizovtseva, a secretary of the Moscow *gorkom,* is the deputy Chair of the committee.

The pattern of women's CC representation strongly supports the argument that it is planned and controlled. The consistency in the percentage of women on the one hand, and their selection from either a narrow range of low-status occupations or party and official posts on the other, has ensured that the sex factor remains a feature of the CC. The *nomenklatura* process is a factor governing female entry to the party hierarchy. Whether or not women want to participate in political power, factors of control exist outside of women's wishes.

SOVIET ATTITUDES

The *nomenklatura,* as part of the party structure, is in turn affected by attitudes within the party. We now turn to these attitudes to help us understand further why so little change has occurred for women in the party leadership over the past thirty years. The scarcity of material on Soviet women's political culture means that much is necessarily conjecture. Surveys have suggested that women show less interest in politics than men[13] and some Western sources have made this assumption[14]. Soviet sources partially place the blame on women themselves. Ol'ga Tallya (1971, pp.178-9) in reference to women's lack of political expertise, says that female party members are too passive in party organisation and not sufficiently interested in raising their political-ideological level.

The lack of women in high office does not appear to worry women themselves. The response of one Moscow acquaintance to enquiry about the omission of women from the politburo was, 'Oh, Aren't there any? Well, that's not a matter of concern'. There is a commonsense notion that women do not need to be in positions of political power. Benevolent paternalism is regarded as adequate for achieving sexual equality. This attitude was clearly demonstrated by a Soviet physicist during a visit to London in 1981. When questioned about women's political position, she responded to the effect that the main legislation for sexual equality was introduced after the 1917 revolution by men. This support for equality renders equal representation by women unnecessary.

The impression that such attitudes are widespread was borne out by Tat'yana Sidirova who agreed about the disinterest, maintaining that 'nobody is bothered by it, not even women.' Her explanations were twofold. Firstly, as the Central Committee includes people specialising in 'women's problems' and party policy reflects this, there is no acute necessity for a woman in the politburo to deal with women's problems. All that is objectively possible is being done already. Secondly, whilst she accepted that an equal representation of women at all levels of party organisation would indicate real equal status in society, she argued that the bite was taken out of this point by women's participation on a mass scale at other levels. Given that women are so socially and politically active, there is little to worry about.

We have argued, though, that the sexual division in political power is a crucial factor affecting women's status. Without full participation, political systems are only 'democratic' in a limited sense. Authoritative claims that equal rights have been implemented in full continue to appear from time to time, but it is now widely accepted in the USSR that equal rights between the sexes are not fully exercised. Although commonsense notions appear not to associate full political representation with equality, official calls are made for the active promotion of women.

Official attitudes to such promotion have gone through

various stages. In the post-revolutionary period, women's active participation was encouraged. With the abolition of the party's women's department, the *zhenotdel*, this became little more than paper policy. The assertion that women were now equal to men, prevented analysis of the low female participation. The Khrushchev era recognised that there was no automatic relationship between legislation and practice. Criticism was particularly sharp during this time, as in the speech of a delegate to a conference for party cadres (1958):

> In our *oblast'* conferences we always advocate and then record as a decision, that the *obkom* of the party must engage in training and involve women in leadership work. But the decisions are not fulfilled. We now have one woman secretary of the CC and some ministers. A short while ago the situation was as follows. There were women on the *obkom* buro, there was a woman secretary of the *obkom*, women were heads and assistant heads of party departments and there were four ministers. But what is the situation now? There is not one woman on the buro of the *obkom*, there are neither secretaries nor heads of departments, nor assistant heads. Women who are now in leading party work were mainly nominated in the war or early post war years. But where are the nominations now? One, two, that's all. Ask yourselves, if women in the war years were able to take the place of men in difficult responsibilities, if they were able to cope with the difficult areas of work in the first post war years, then why can't they do so now? (*Partiinaya Zhizn*, No. 5, 1958, pp.45-7).

Since Khrushchev, there has been a steady stream of resolutions calling for improvement. A pattern emerged of initial congratulation both to women and party for the advances made, followed by reference to the continuing low level of female participation, yet to reach its 'optimum level' (Litvinova & Popova, 1975, p.10). During the 1970s there was evidence of a renewal of concern. Official calls echoing Khrushchev[15], were made for the more active promotion of women, such as that contained in Brezhnev's speech at his last congress: 'It has to be acknowledged that so far not all possibilities are being used to promote women to executive posts. This must be corrected' (Brezhnev, 23 February 1981). Five years later, at the 27th Party Congress, Mikhail Gorbachev has added his voice with 'More women should be more vigorously promoted to party posts' (Resolution on the Political Report, 6 March 1986).

More space about women in the party was allotted in party writings. In 1976, the first secretary of Kalushevskii *obkom* dispensed with the habitual single paragraph on women to include biographical details and comment on women holding posts of responsibility in the region. He emphasised the importance of the posts and hoped that the success of these women would encourage others (Kondrenikov, 1976, p.131). In Ivanovo, the textile region where female workers predominate, an *obkom* plenum, 'On Improving Work Amongst Women', held in conjunction with International Women's Year, was marked by its sharp criticism of the lack of progress (*Partiinaya Zhizn* No. 16, 1975, pp.39-45).

General writings on women, however, continue to make favourable comparison of Soviet women with their counterparts in the West by reference to government participation (Mollaeva, 1978, p.57). Reference to women in the CPSU is marked by its generality, such as 'Many female communists are chosen for leading party posts, and they successfully cope with their task' (Kotelenetz, 1977, p.226). There is little evidence of change in this approach. Biryukova provides data, in 1985, to support the extensive participation of women in the soviets, but returns to generalisation in respect to party committees, 'Women have been elected to leading bodies of the party . . .' (Biryukova, 1985, p.310).

This statistical generality does evoke criticism however. Academic theses during the 1970s, concerned with the theme of female political participation, are a source of critical appraisal of the CPSU in its relation to women. In keeping with Soviet social science much of the criticism is empirically based, but this in itself is an attempt to make women more visible. Zhvirble for example, criticising statistical generality, asked for more detailed analysis to replace the usual 'including women'. As she rightly points out, without knowledge of the actual position, improvement is difficult (Zhvirble, 1980, pp.178-9). Zhvirble herself begins this process with data on the occupational backgrounds of women in 120 party organisations in Moscow and Latvia. From this she found that 'The party stratum of working women is still far lower amongst women than men, for example in machine building' (*ibid.*, p.178).

Another area justifying criticism by Soviet academics is women's political education[16]. Attendance at the Higher Party School has been identified as a route to party careers, with 80 per cent of graduates being recommended for posts of responsibility (Bialer, 1980, p.178). As Jancar has pointed out (1978, p.114) the lack of skills taught at party schools restricts women's party career. Tallya, writing in 1971, stressed the inadequacy of women's political education. During 1974-7 however, the number of women attending party schools at all levels doubled from 12 per cent to 24 per cent, and is therefore commensurate with their party membership (Cheidene, 1980, p.45). Cheidene considers that this increase is due directly to measures taken by the CPSU enabling women to take part in 'systematic and deep study of Marxist Leninist theory so that they can be promoted'[17]. However, Cheidene is referring to resolutions on women's party political education passed in 1968, whereas it is these resolutions that Tallya complains had had no effect. Zhvirble (1980, p.180) still considers that the system of party education for women needs further improvement, and refers specifically to fitting women for posts at *raikom* and *obkom* level, but no higher.

Official calls for promotion of women to 'executive' posts so far have been little more than empty rhetoric. Attention to the question of female participation remains limited in two respects. Firstly, it fails to address the marginality of women in political power, and secondly, it fails to recognise that this failure arises from Soviet theory itself.

Soviet Responses and Explanations
Although Soviet authorities highlight the differences between political participation in the USSR and the West, their explanations of low female participation bear a marked similarity to many Western ones[18]. Official Soviet explanations are threefold. Firstly the sexual division of labour which gives women the major responsibility for family and home (Zhvirble, 1980, p.52). This allows them less time than men to devote to socio-political activities[19]. Secondly, traditional attitudes towards women persist and lead to some sexual discrimination[20]. Thirdly, women themselves: in some cases female political consciousness still falls below that of men (Slai-

shcheva, 1978, p.27), and women's own attitudes present a 'psychological barrier' (Ivanovo Plenum, *Partiinaya Zhizn*, No. 16, 1975 pp.39-45).

The corresponding policies put forward by party and state emphasise the importance of time. The main panacea is to alleviate female roles in the sexual division of labour so that women can perform their new public roles more effectively. 'If women are to be party cadres, then they must be cared for as wife, mother and citizen, by improving their living conditions' (Cheidene, 1980, p.12). Public facilities and technology in the home are to be extended (Zhvirble, 1980, pp.179-80). This simply awaits sufficient development of the Soviet economy. 'We consider that the general improvement of living conditions in the future, the strengthening of state and social care for the education of children will allow in the near future and will secure, the active promotion of women to leading managerial and social political life' (Kondrenikov, 1976, p.134).

Great faith is invested in this solution. Sidirova, in her interview, expressed unease at raising the percentage of women in posts artificially. 'Life should be such that women of their own accord, in a natural way, ascend to leading positions.' For her too, the way that this could occur was for the needs of everyday life to be met.

> When our everyday services are at a much higher level, and our party and the 26th congress have paid serious attention to this question, to the food supply, improvement of everyday services, better housing conditions so that every family gets a separate flat with all modern conveniences, more kindergartens to more fully satisfy the population's demand for pre-school institutions . . . . So, all these questions, when they are all settled completely, and the home front catches them up, then of course, you'll see how our women will surge forward. (Sidirova, Moscow, 1981).

The implications of this policy are rarely questioned although, as Lapidus has shown, alternative approaches do exist (Lapidus, 1978, pp.324-34). Ol'ga Tallya for example, makes the pertinent point in her thesis that the provision of washing machines might lighten women's work, but does not remove their responsibility for the washing (Tallya, 1971, p.204). She emphasises that male roles must be changed if women are to devote more time to social and political activities (p.216) insisting that women should have equal free time to men *(ibid.,* p.199)[21].

Discrimination by men has been recognised since the Khrushchev era, although it is generally perceived as an individual problem, not a societal one. Reference is made to the folk norm that women are less easy to work with than men (Kadeikan *et al.,* 1974, p.193). Cheidene's thesis refers to the 'conservative attitude to women' amongst Latvian ministers and others, which expresses itself in the belief that 'women are unsuitable for independent work'. It is this, not women's inadequacy which prevents their promotion (Cheidene, 1980, pp.218-9). General policy to change male attitudes remains muted, despite official condemnation of sexual discrimination. There is little evidence of more than the occasional campaign and appeals for men to assist women more in the home and share parental responsibilities. The implicit assumption that women have the main responsibility for children and the home remains virtually unchallenged.

A continuing theme refers to the lower cultural level of women with its accompanying level of consciousness. The initial comparison between male and female literacy rates no longer applies, with the greater proportion of women having higher education than men. Now, religious belief is the factor used (Mollaeva, 1978, p.61). The party's agitation and propaganda departments, the media and the zhensovety are urged to improve political education amongst women with anti-religious activity[22]. But Zhvirble (1980, p.51) maintains that the high level of women's educational achievements makes them now ready to fulfil the 'high duty of a communist'. She proposes that women would now benefit from the practical experience of work in the party, this being the most effective means for raising female activity and responsibility (Zhvirble, 1980, p.166). Such proposals are marked by their rarity and limitation to the lower levels of party organisation.

Soviet explanations fail to consider ideology as a contributory factor. Lenin's dictum that socialism is impossible without the full participation of women is often quoted as the linch pin on which to hang the existence of their equality (Litvinova & Popova, 1975, p.5). As socialism is presumed to exist, so must the equality of women. Sometimes the tautology of the argument is clearly evident: 'It would have been impossible to turn women into full and equal participants in social construction without promoting their social and political activity and involving them in the administration of the state and all public affairs' (Yemelyanova, 1975, p.41)[23].

Thus according to Soviet political theory, women's 'full and equal participation in socialist construction' proves that women are also politically active. To question the logicality of this is to question the basic tenet of Soviet theory on women's politicisation. Yet this is indeed what began to happen. The greater realism which emerged under Khrushchev necessarily found itself at odds with existing theory. Brezhnev's concept of 'mature socialism' provided an escape route for this dilemma, it enabled the time scale to be extended. The proof of socialism is no longer dependent on the actual equality of women, it is now 'advanced socialism' which will be the stage for the 'full factual equality of women' (Kalinina, 1980, p.18). The concept does not resolve the theoretical dilemma, though.

It has been argued by feminists in the West that for women to participate requires strong images of women in relevant positions. Moses suggests that this has had an influence on the high number of women in ideological posts (Moses, in Atkinson *et al.*, 1978, p.351). Images of women in posts of responsibility are a regular feature of women's journals and the media in general. This suggests that the importance of role models is recognised in the USSR. Most images depict women in production, such as Vera Golubeva *(Rabotnitsa,* No. 11, 1981) or the highly competent public figure who besides being a mother, possesses the feminine attributes of being well dressed, and well groomed. Valentina Nikolaeva-Tereshkova, for example, is described as 'Cosmonaut, active in public work, deputy, member of Supreme Soviet Presidium, happy mother, wife and housekeeper' *(Krest'yanka,* 1975, No. 10, p.3)[24]. Most images are of women in low political positions because that is where they are. This represents a chicken and egg situation. With so few women in prominent positions there are few models to emulate. With the *nomenklatura* system, the CPSU is in a unique position to intervene in the promulgation of role models. Whilst there is no guarantee that such appointments would of themselves lead to greater female participation, it is not evident that the party has yet seriously tried this as a strategy. On the contrary, the promotion of such small numbers of women is subject to the criticism of 'tokenism' (Jancar, 1978, p.103; also Moses, 1978; and Salaff and Merkle, 1970, p.177). Whilst this is a valid point, it does not undermine the virtue of trying out a policy of appointing women commensurate with their party membership, as a first step, to act as role models for other women. Without that the image of women in the public sphere itself fails to challenge the traditional image which associates males with positions of power. Such 'positive' images of women which exist already are countered by models which present women as 'politically naive and passive' (Rosenham, in Atkinson *et al.*, 1978, pp.196-7).

Underlying Soviet responses is the deeply held, and as yet unchallenged, belief that female biology determines gender roles. In particular women's maternal role frequently occurs as explanation. This is made explicit in an article celebrating International Women's Year.

It should be borne in mind that women are drawn into socio-political activity *to the extent that it will not prevent them from fulfilling their prime social function, that of being mothers*. Therefore the proportion of women in the party, the soviets and trade union bodies, and especially those holding high elective posts, is smaller than that of men. (Yemelyanova in Danilova *et al.*, 1975, p.68) (my emphasis).

Ol'ga Tallya (1971, p.68), despite her protestations on women's behalf, likewise has to be seen in such a context, for she quotes Krupskaya's oft repeated belief that 'women have an innate maternal instinct, thus it is they who will inevitably have the leading role in child care'. This places Tallya's remarks referred to above within the context that women's biology determines their gender roles. It is not surprising therefore to find it strongly reiterated in commonsense notions. A male PhD student acquaintance, for example, maintained that if women were to enter leading posts they would have to take on 'male characteristics' (Moscow, 1981).

The conflation of the gender roles of caring and rearing of

children, with the biological one of bearing, prevents the goals of women's political advance from equalling those of men. This is the underlying paradigm giving rise to Soviet responses to women in politics. The remedies proposed are therefore designed to enable women to fulfil their gender roles more adequately, not to change female and male gender roles fundamentally. Official Soviet commitment to equality has failed to provide an adequate alternative to the underlying 'biologism'. Once Soviet authorities had admitted that equality has yet to be achieved, reasons had to be sought. Biologism emerged as the unstated explanation. It prevents implementation of the economic remedies proposed over the last thirty years. Indeed, by reiterating that it is women who require assistance in the home, the existing division of labour is reinforced. Until the generality of the problem is recognised, it will remain an integral part of Soviet society. Hence its sexism. The institutionalisation of separate male and female models which perpetuate rather than undermine the images of traditional gender roles, is a feature of this sexism.

It is evident that under-participation of women does receive attention. It features in official pronouncements, amongst party activists and as a topic for academic research. It has borne fruit with the increase in participation, reflected in female party membership and posts up to *obkom* level. The main criteria for further improvement lean heavily towards increasing aid to women for the rationalisation of their private roles. Awareness of discrimination in the main remains at the level of the individual. More attention is given to raising women's political culture. Images of active public figures are presented in the media, but countered by traditional images. There are few attempts to utilise women's higher cultural level by developing political skills.

There is less evidence of concern about low female representation in the party hierarchy, or of the *nomenklatura* implementing the calls to put women into executive posts. The increase in party membership in Kirghizia, and the electoral pattern, strongly suggests that whatever reluctance exists on the part of women to participate in politics, women could be found if required. In the thirty or so years since women's low participation was openly raised, the party has only intervened at those levels which do not constitute a serious inroad into political power, the power held by males. The virtual silence of the leadership, its lack of serious analysis, marks discriminatory practice against women. The position of the CPSU as the 'vanguard' of Soviet society makes the denial of women in the power positions of that vanguard a discriminatory practice which can only serve to perpetuate their inequality. The reason for this institutionalised discrimination by the CPSU is revealed in the ideology which underlines Soviet responses to women's political situation. Women are primarily considered as mothers. Policy reflects this. There is tacit acceptance of the biological basis of existing gender roles. To deny women in practice equal access to political power is sexist discrimination.

This study addresses the question of whether the wide participation of women in 'low' and informal political structures can sufficiently raise political consciousness to challenge such attitudes. According to Soviet political theory, informal political activity, in particular in the public, voluntary 'social' organisations, is the proving ground for the development of such a political consciousness. 'Participation in social work is how interest in the collective in region, republic and state affairs will be raised' (Tallya, 1975, p.19). It is in these 'mass' organisations that the skills which women are considered to lack are to be learned and tested. Yet the data presented in this chapter show that this professed relationship between the formal and informal has not been realised. The following chapters will look at the activity of women in their 'social' organisations to find out why there has been such little effective challenge to existing party practices.

NOTES

1. Ronald Hill and Peter Frank (1981, pp.141, 144), discuss the problems associated with this concept and its rejection by Soviet theorists.
2. Bohdan Harasymiw (1969, p.511) has estimated that three million administrative and executive posts in official bodies came under its jurisdiction.

    The election of female deputies shows a particularly clear pattern. The proportion of women in the soviets has not only steadily advanced, but with a uniformity common to all regions despite differing socio-economic development. In 1975, for example, the percentage of women elected at local level ranged from 44.8 per cent to 49.4 per cent. Similarly, the percentage of female deputies with party membership ranged between 40 per cent and 48 per cent. See Lapidus (1978) Table 22, p.206.
3. Whereas Jancar (1978, p.103) has argued that the party has the power—'if it really wanted women in positions of political power, it would put them there'—Mickiewicz (1977, p.422) has suggested that planning by the CPSU is not centrally controlled, and recognition of the regional patterns provides a better base for understanding the patterns of female participation. Hill and Frank (1981, p.43) have calculated that at an annual rate of increase of 3.8 per cent, it would take women to the year 2043 to reach half the present party membership, and only if all male recruitment ceased.
4. The Kirghiz advance followed a CC resolution (September 1976), which called on party organisations to pay particular attention to women and youth *(KPSS v Resoluziyakh* T.12, p.364, quoted in Zhvirble, 1980, p.73). There have been similar resolutions directed to other party organisations, for example, 'On the work of the Communist Party of Tadzhikistan in fulfilling the decisions of the 23rd Congress of the CPSU' which criticised the local party for failing to raise women's consciousness sufficiently for them to join the party (quoted in Zhvirble, 1980, p.72).
5. For detailed information on party structure see Hill and Frank (1981) Ch. 3.
6. See also Harasymiw, in Yedlin ed. (1980) Table 10:12, p.173.
7. This also applies to the soviets despite the greater number of women participating. Of the 550 deputy ministers and deputy Chair of the ministries and state committees of the USSR Council of Ministers (1975), only seven were female. In the post-war period only two USSR ministries have been held by women: Culture and Health. The RSFSR has had a female Minister of Social Security since 1952. Hough (in Atkinson *et al.*, 1978, pp.363-6) shows that women on committeees tend to confine their contributions to these same areas.
8. This point is made by both Soviet and Western sources: see *Soviet Life* magazine (3 March 1974) and Harasymiw in Yedlin ed. (1980, p.168). It was also emphasised in the interview with Tat'yana Sidirova.

9. In the autonomous republics of Mordoi, Mari and Chuvash, 50 per cent of all propagandists in the early 1970s were female. Tallya (1971, p.68). In Moscow and Latvia in 1977-9 70 per cent of the 'ideological organisers' were female, Zhvirble (1980, p.164). See also Moses' research of 'indoctrination posts' in the RSFSR and Ukraine in Atkinson *et al.* (1978, p.340).
10. Zhvirble (1980, Table 7, p.163) shows that amongst the staff of the *Detskii Mir* children's store in Moscow, women fulfil all the tasks of the 'ideological commission'. Female party members as a total of all party members active in the store's agitprop are as follows: propaganda—100 per cent; leaders of schools—100 per cent; lecturers—100 per cent; political information—83 per cent.
11. For details of composition see Hough and Fainsod (1979), Table 32, p.459.
12. O. P. Kol'china as second secretary Moscow *obkom* 1960-3; L. P. Lykova second secretary Ivanovo *obkom* until 1955, then second secretary Smolensk *obkom* 1958-61; Z. M. Kruglova, as secretary Leningrad *obkom* 1968-74.
13. See Stephen White (1979) who refers to research by Artiinan, Grishan and Ermiratskii.
    See also L. V. Ostapenko (1974).
14. Jancar (1978, p.200) refers to the 'apolitical consciousness' of Soviet women. This presumes, not necessarily correctly, that women who participate in the political institutions do so for reasons of conformity rather than political commitment. This notion finds echo in Moses (Atkinson *et al.*, 1978, p.351), as explanation for the high proportion of girls and young women who are secretaries of the *Komsomol* [the youth organisation of the Communist Party].
15. Compare this with Nikita Khrushchev (1956), 'Many Party and soviet bodies exhibit timidity about putting women into executive posts' *Pravda* (15 February 1956), quoted in Currell (1974, p.129).
16. Tallya (1971, p.178) gives the example of a candidate member of the party who failed to become a full member owing to insufficient attention to her education by the Chebosarskii *raion* (Chuvash ASSR).
17. Tallya (1971, p.184) quotes a resolution passed by the Chuvash *obkom* in 1968: 'The situation in promoting and educating women cadres in the republic'. It noted the 'serious insufficiencies' both within the CPSU and the ministries in promoting women to leadership posts. A similar resolution was passed in Mari ASSR on 31 May 1968 (Tallya, 1971, p.182).
18. Jeane Kirkpatrick (1974, p.4) for example, cites four main 'hypothetical constraints': physiological, cultural, role and male discrimination. Useful summaries and critiques of biological explanations are provided by Laurel Walum (1976) and S. M. Okin (1980), Feminists have increasingly turned to concepts of 'institutionalised sexism'. See for example, Frieda Gehlens, 'Women Members of Congress: a distinctive role' in Githens and Prestage eds. (1977).
19. Age patterns give credence to the importance of gender roles. Young

women are active in the *Komsomol* and return to public activity in their forties and fifties (Moses, 1978, p.350). However, Cheidene (1980, p.166) notes that women are beginning to return earlier, between the ages of thirty-five and forty. Women deputies are also being elected at an earlier age, women under forty-five years now being nominated on a 1:1 ratio compared to 1:10 for women over forty-five years of age (Maher in Yedlin ed., 1980, p.192).

20. Nina Yakimenko, *Pravda* (7 August 1961) in discussing the draft party programme, refers to female leaders being met with 'hostile glances'. The Turkmenian discussion of the 22nd Congress CPSU *(Pravda,* 14 January 1962) refers to the 'hidden resistance' of some communists to the promotion of women to leading posts.

21. There is some evidence of the party re-educating men, especially in the Central Asian republics. El'darova (1963, p.68) for example, refers to Agul'skii raion (Daghestan) where the party and *Komsomol* have actively encouraged young fathers to take part in housework.

22. See also Annanurova (1968, p.4); Novikova *et al.* (1978, p.74); and Yemelyanova, 'The social and political activity of Soviet women' in Danilova *et al.* (1975, p.69).

23. Such attitudes are popularised by 'leading' figures like Valentina Nikolaeva-Tereshkova: 'Participation in socially productive work . . . moulds their [women's] civic and political maturity' (trans. *CDSP*, Vol. XXVII, No. 9, 1975).

24. Mollie Schwartz Rosenham has shown that women are depicted in children's primary readers as 'politically naive and passive'. Rosenham, 'Images of Male and Female in Children's Readers' in Atkinson *et al.* (1978, pp.196-7). Hough (1978, p.365) suggests that women are 'not perceived as political'.

3 Informal Political Activity: The 'Social' Organisations

Informal political activity in the 'mass' organisations is an integral part of the Soviet political network. These voluntary 'social'[1] organisations have responsibility for various aspects of Soviet society, but are themselves accountable to the formal political institutions of the government and CPSU. The high representation of women in this form of activity means many issues from the private sphere have found acceptability in the public. As the previous chapter showed though, neither these sex-specific issues, nor women themselves, have progressed to higher politics. As Barbara Wolfe Jancar (1978, p.111) says, women's influence '. . . appears to be indirect at best, localized and focussed on specific "women's issues" '. Thus one of the problematics about a broad concept of political activity is the link between formal and informal politics. The informal area has remained relegated, and with it 'women's issues' are marginalised. Detailed investigation into the zhensovety, the women-only 'social' organisations, attempts to show why this remains so.

THE 'SOCIAL' ORGANISATIONS

The 'social' organisations came into prominence under Khrushchev[2]. To distinguish themselves from the Stalin era, the new leadership proposed greater public involvement. 'Participatory democracy', highlighted at the 21st Party Congress became one of the key themes. 'The Congress notes that in contemporary conditions, the main aim, is to draw all citizens into participation on the supervision of productive and cultural construction, in the management of social activities' (Mitskevich, 1959, p.24)[3]. It was the 'social' organisations, together with the soviets and their commissions which, according to Khrushchev in his report on the 1961 Programme of the CPSU *(Soviet Booklet,* No. 81, 1961), were to further this process: 'The advance of socialist democracy is bound up with a heightening of the social organisations'. This voluntary participation was seen as returning to the Leninist maxim that 'every cook shall govern', unequivocally stated by Khrushchev as: 'What will remain with the withering away of the state? The social organisations' (quoted in Mitskevich, 1959, p.26)[4].

Alongside an extension of democracy, the role of the CPSU was to be strengthened. 'In the new stage of our development, it is especially important to improve the party leadership of the soviets and the economic, trades unions, YCL, co-op and other mass organisations' (Khrushchev, 18 October 1961, *Soviet Booklet* No. 81, p.59). Leadership by the CPSU did not entail a formalised, structural relationship. It meant that all these institutions worked within the political culture of the party. The very concept of self-government was associated with communist society, 'participation in community self-help organisation results . . . in learning the skills and habits of communist self-government'[5].

The 'social' organisations are thereby conceived as political. In his speech to the 21st Congress CPSU, Voroshilov dubbed them 'a school for communism' (quoted in Mitskevitch, *Sovetskoe Gosydarstvo i pravo,* No. 9, p.27). Thus their areas of concern, such as 'order in the environment' and child care provision, became defined as political activity[6]. Given this role of 'social' organisations, the existence of the zhensovety poses the following question. As 'social' organisations act within the parameters of communist party theory and policy, can the zhensovety, who have particular responsibility for women, participate on behalf of women even where that might not coincide with that theory and policy?

An assessment involves interpretation of the concept of 'participation'[7]. 'Controlled' participation does not mean it is not 'authentic' (Bialer, 1980, p.186). It is not inevitably a one-way process, despite any difficulty this notion might present to presumptions about Soviet participation made from Western values. As Friedgut has suggested, citizens' 'social' organisations may well benefit citizens by enabling them to have facilities they would otherwise lack (Friedgut, 1979, p.242). The same author has also suggested that participation patterns may eventually influence the Soviet political system *(ibid.,* p.289). As Christel Lane (1981) has shown in her work on religion and ritual, one role of the 'social' organisations is to influence non-hegemonic cultures. Zhensovety activity in this respect will show that one method is to incorporate counter and sub-cultural elements, with the possible result that aspects of these enter the prevailing hegemony[8].

There has been speculation that the 'social' organisations have undergone some change since Khrushchev, with the Brezhnev era being more concerned with mobilisation than the development of citizen skills for the 'withering away of the state' (Friedgut, 1979, p.65). The functional role of mobilisation for the solidarity of society is made clear in a Soviet reference to the zhensovety: 'through social organisations, the definitive social structure is raised . . . a form of uniting people ' (Yatrol'skaya, 1972). There are indications, however, of a renewed interest in their participatory role. Cheidene (1980, p.113) quotes Brezhnev's reference to the place in communist self-government made at the 22nd Party Congress[9]. Andropov specifically referred to the 'social' organisations, including the 'women's organisations', as presenting 'possibilities for further democratisation'[10]. This has since been reiterated by Gorbachev, in his report on the 1986 Programme of the CPSU 'The Party attaches priority significance to augmenting the role of the public organisations—important parts of the system of the people's socialist self government' *(Soviet News,* 19 March 1986).

Despite policy changes, the growth of 'social' organisations has continued unabated. In the mid-1960s, 966,412 organisations existed with a membership of 9,724,372, approximately 7 per cent of the electorate (Chkhikvadze, 1965, p.88). By 1979, not counting the 2.2 million deputies, 30,000,000 citizens were involved[11].

Whatever the actual interpretation of participation at any

given time, the 'social' organisations remain the means by which the party aims to extend its contact with Soviet citizens for the purpose of building a communist society orchestrated by the CPSU.

THE ZHENSOVETY

The Khrushchev leadership acknowledged both a lack of commitment amongst sections of the population and the need to tackle this to realise the plan of 'Communism by the 1980s'. The strengthening of the CPSU and the development of participatory democracy through the 'social' organisations were necessary to achieve this. A policy of 'differentiation' was introduced to effect these aims[12]. This policy distinguished between differing social categories, recognising their distinctive characteristics. One such group was women. This returned to the practice of the early post-revolutionary years, which had supported a women's section in the party. The *zhenotdel* achieved much, but was disbanded in 1930 on the grounds that it was no longer needed—women had acquired equality therefore no longer represented a distinct social category with separate needs. It was not until Khrushchev's wind of change that it could be admitted that this was not so.

There are probably two main reasons for this volte face. To strengthen its influence the party was required to make more effective use of agitprop (agitation and propaganda). Women, especially housewives, were detected as a sector of the population where that influence was markedly low. In Leningrad for example, the agitprop department of the *obkom* acknowledged that 'we have recognised that citizens exist who for this or that reason, are not influenced by ideological work, who do not attend lectures . . . especially women workers and housewives ' (Sapozhnikov, 1962, p.451)[13]. The second factor was Khrushchev's plans for 'Communism by the 1980s' which demanded more women in production. Despite past mobilisation, a significant proportion of women remained economically inactive. During this period, thirteen million people entered the work force, 'most of whom were women' *(Literaturnaya Gazetta,* 16 May 1979, p.13).

Extending the influence of the party's political culture amongst women became a feature of its literature at this time. Women's education was to be a visible part of propaganda work, with lectures and talks both more frequent and at a higher political level[14]. Women in particular were influenced by the counter-culture of religion (Il'chieva, *Kommunist,* No. 14, 1959, p.47) so were to be prised away to enable the party to maximise its own influence[15]. There are a number of signs that the policy of differentiation was put into effect. In a number of regions women's congresses date from this time, the first Uzbek women's congress took place in 1958, as did meetings for women. Chelyabinsk steel works for example, held its first for 'many years' (Pavlova and Cheryadeva in Kuznetsova ed., 1961, p.23).

The zhenotdel and its 'delegatki' had recognised that women's political and social consciousness would best be facilitated by the support of other women. Their success provided a pointer to how the differentiated approach could be implemented under Khrushchev. Despite the evident lack of an official blueprint proposing women-only groups, it is the zhensovety which gradually find favour. Throughout the late 1950s and early 1960s they are referred to in party articles with increasing frequency, eventually being adopted as the most suitable and successful form of activity for working with women[16].

It could be expected that the promotion of women-only groups would present Soviet theorists with a dilemma. Indeed, the staff member interviewed at *Rabotnitsa* agreed that this volte face had caused some embarrassment. On the one hand it was deemed necessary to treat women as a separate category. On the other, the removal of class conflict is supposed to have removed that need—the structural base exists for sexual equality. In an attempt to avoid this potential dilemma, women's participation in 'social' organisations was interpreted by some as an expression of their equality, rather than the means of realising that equality: 'one of the decisive conditions of the existence of full equal rights for women is apparent in their wide involvement in socially useful work'

(Chkhikvadze, 1965, p.129). This ignored the frequent references by the zhensovety to their task of developing those skills which women lacked compared to men.

A number of responses to the zhensovety show that the policy of women-only groups was not universally accepted. There is scepticism about their value, and rejection of their need. In Simferopol' the response to the zhensovety was: 'There's a strong party organisation in the factory, the factory committee works well, why is a zhensovet required as well? (Borisova, 1956, p.3). (A similar reaction is noted by A. P. Polegeshko, 1961, p.6). In Odessa, the zhensovet report says its formation was met with a 'condescending smile' (Babkova in Polishchuk, 1964). Such attitudes have continued. More recently there have been recommendations to disband the zhensovety. Tallya (1975, p.64) refers to party workers who think the zhensovety have now outlived their use—something which she strongly rejects[17].

Why the zhensovety should be the preferred form of work amongst women is a matter of speculation. It is probable that one reason lies in the previous ineffectiveness of party work amongst women, thereby discrediting any form associated with it. It is also possible that the party shake-up following Stalin favoured a break with previous methods of work, wherever possible. In this case a new, or apparently new, form of work would be more acceptable. In addition, the emphasis on 'participatory democracy' required organisations which could be seen to reflect this policy. The structural independence of the zhensovety gave them an advantage in this respect over the party's Departments for Work Amongst Women.

A further explanation can be deduced from zhensovety reports. Any policy showing renewed interest in women undoubtedly referred to the work of the *zhenotdel*. Its success had been acknowledged in promoting not only literacy but female politicisation. Whilst it is true that the *zhenotdel* had been formally attached to the CPSU, it had two special features. One was that it was women only, the other was its network of *'delegatki'* who worked collectively with women throughout the USSR. The zhensovety are referred to as the 'spiritual heirs' of the *zhenotdel* and its *delegatki*. 'The assemblies of women delegates have been revived today in the form of the zhensovety' (Tatarinova, 1968, p.97). 'The spirit of the "red kerchiefs" is embodied today in the activists of the zhensovety . . . at their conferences, congresses and meetings, their members and their voluntary helpers are today's "red kerchiefs" ' *(Otchizna,* March 1981). The similarity in much of the work of the two organisations is illustrated by description of their activities in Uzbekistan (Aminova, 1977).

Association of the zhensovety with the zhenotdel was useful to the Khrushchev leadership. The zhenotdel had had the support of Lenin. As Nasriddinova (1964, p.146) says about the formation of the zhensovety, 'the Soviet state is now returning to this excellent idea of Lenin's'. This gave the post-Stalin leadership an acceptable authority by which to legitimise the policy of 'differentiation'. Writings on the zhensovety continue to make frequent reference to Lenin's authority.

The most systematic information about the zhensovety comes from the period 1958-61 which can be dated as their main growth period[18]. By the early 1960s they were already widespread, involving many thousands of women[19]. They are located in the workplace and in residential areas. They exist at the level of village, town, district, region and republic. They now predominate in rural communities such as that found in Moldavia, which had 2,000 in 1978 *(Krest'yanka,* No. 10, 1978, p.23); autonomous republics of minority nationalities like Chuvash—1,700 in 1978 *(Krest'yanka,* No. 11, 1978, p.22); and regions of strong religious influence—Catholic Lithuania had 4,000 zhensovety in 1975 (Dirzhinskaiete, 1975a, p.28), and in the Muslim region of Tadzhikistan there were 1,310 in 1980 *(Rabotnitsa,* No. 11, 1980). The zhensovety thus predominate in those regions where women's social status is considered to be the most impeded by tradition and level of economic and cultural development, in other words where consciousness most needs to be raised[20].

Zhensovety Characteristics
Since the 1960s, then, women have had access to women-only groups. Other bodies dealing specifically with women's issues also exist. But the zhensovety have a number of charac-

teristics which distinguish them from these. Characterisation of the zhensovety as 'independent organisations whose activists work on their own initiative' (Moskvina, correspondence, 1980), arises from the lack of formal structure to other bodies. This distinguishes them from other women-only organisations which have emerged since the Khrushchev period: the 'Commissions for Work Amongst Women' which are trades union bodies, and the standing commissions 'On the Problems of Labour and Everyday Life of Women and for Mother and Child Protection' which are attached to the soviets. Both refer back directly to male colleagues. Zhensovety independence is underlined by such descriptions as, 'spontaneous groups which are unofficial'; their 'ad hoc' nature (Stites, 1978, p.414), and that they 'operate independently of one another' (Hansson and Liden, 1984, p.84). These features are reflected in zhensovety activity and structure, which are described as flexible, responding to the 'specific features and conditions of development of a given republic' (Danilova *et al.*, 1975, p.67), and to the local women (Makeeva, in Koldova ed., 1961, p.4). This contrasts with the Soviet Women's Committee, the most familiar representative of Soviet women to us in the West. This is an appointed body which exists only at national level, headed by a prominent woman, at present the cosmonaut Valentina Nikolaeva-Tereshkova, whose primary role is to make contact with women's organisations abroad. It arose as an anti-fascist body in the 1940s. The zhensovety however, are local organisations, widespread throughout the USSR, involving thousands of Soviet women, via elected committees. The form of zhensovety also differs from all the other bodies. The groups are small, enabling them to be described as 'an organ of collective thought' (Nasriddinova, 1964, p.170).

The aims of the zhensovety also mark their difference from the other organisations by being more specifically political. Their aim is to raise women's political activity and teach them political skills (Rutyantseva *et al.*, 1963, p.15) in the context of raising women's general political consciousness (Zaripova, 1965, p.32). The trades union commissions are more work-specific. The zhensovety also have a supportive role. This takes two main forms. Firstly, to ease women's daily lives by practical help, a role emphasised by Richard Stites (1978, pp.414-5): 'Their purpose is for bettering the conditions of life . . . by means of inspections, evaluations and recommendations'. The second is to provide personal support, in the words of one activist 'The zhensovety must speak up in defence of women and girls by exposing the survival of "feudal attitudes" to women' *(Osvobozhenaya zhenshchina Sovetskovo Vostoka,* 1972, p.99).

These characteristics of the zhensovety appear similar to criteria found supportive for raising consciousness by Western women's groups. There are parallels in the definition of social and voluntary activities on women's issues as political, as is the description of the zhensovety as 'independent', women-only organisations, with the important feature of autonomy. Both these aspects of the zhensovety will be explored in following chapters. We now look at the zhensovety as 'ad hoc', 'spontaneous' organisations in terms of their origins.

The Zhensovety—'Spontaneous' and 'ad hoc'?
The characterisation of the zhensovety as 'spontaneous', 'ad hoc' women's groups appears to have arisen for two reasons. The first is due to the sporadic emergence of the zhensovety over a period of time. The second is the diverse range of initiatives which led to the formation of individual zhensovet. In terms of consciousness raising, these characteristics will be of interest if their spontaneity results from the initiatives of local women and if their ad hoc nature enables the zhensovety to respond to women's needs. This could enable the zhensovety to be seen as providing a step towards a female collective consciousness and independence.

Although the zhensovety are generally dated from the Khrushchev period[21], there were some in existence before the war and post-war period, possibly a continuance of the *delegatki*. According to two authorities, Ol'ga Tallya and A. S. Stoyankina, the early zhensovety differed from the later ones both in their location and membership. They were mostly in urban rather than rural regions, 'towns and workers settlements' (Tallya, 1971, p.220), 'mostly in the factories . . . in military quarters and in transport' (Stoyankina, 1962, p.6). As Tallya (1971, p.220) points out, these zhensovety did not service the majority of women who at that time lived in rural regions. Their main purpose was to provide support to particular groups of women such as the 'non-working' wives of men in the armed services, technical engineers and officers (Stoyankina, 1962, p.6). A Moscow acquaintance, wife of an army officer, remembers taking her baby with her to zhensovety meetings before the war.

Some zhensovety remained operative during the war. A former soldier, quoted in *Krest'yanka* (No. 1, 1980, p.28) speaks of the enormous role played by the zhensovety and 'maternal care' they gave to the young soldiers in towns during the war. Although Stoyankina seems unaware of post-war zhensovety prior to Khrushchev, the zhensovet in Odessa for example, was formed in 1949 to provide for the wives of the Black Sea Fleet (Koval', 1961, p.4). The 'spontaneous' emergence of some zhensovety is illustrated by their formation in response to particular needs. One of these was the economic contribution made by women during the war and in the post-war period. 'To rebuild the *kolkhoz* "Bolshevik" after the war, the chairman approached a woman activist for help. From then on the militant "Bolshevika" zhensovet arose, as if by itself' *(Krest'yanka,* No 6, 1978, p.18).

Despite these early zhensovety, it is clear from reports that in most regions the zhensovety were a new phenomenon emanating from the policy of differentiation. People did not always know what to expect: 'At the first meeting, it was stressed that they [the activists] would need to go from house to house, to explain just what a zhensovet was, and the kind of activity it would engage in' (Cheremnykh ed., 1964, p.31). The lack of a central directive at any time, and the spasmodic existence of zhensovety prior to this time, both contribute to the description 'ad hoc'.

This was reinforced by the existence of, sometimes preference for, other forms of work amongst women in response to the differentiated approach. The party Departments for Work Amongst Women had continued in some areas after the abolition of the zhenotdel. There is reference to the party's 'Departments for Social and Political Work Amongst Women' and the 'Women's Agencies' as predecessors of the zhensovety (Shitarev, 1961, p.16). But in other regions, as in Saratov, the local party set up a non-salaried 'Department for Work Amongst Women' in 1961 to strengthen the local zhensovet which had been formed earlier. A member of the Moldavian Central Committee in 1959, refers to an apparent confusion about the form work amongst women should take.

But some party committees have incorrectly understood the closing of the gorkom and raikom 'Departments for Work Amongst Women' and stopped working with the zhensovety. It is necessary evidently to re-activate the zhensovety and give them regular help in their task of mobilizing women for active struggle to fulfill the decisions of the party and government. *(Partiinaya Zhizn,* No. 11, 1959, p.24)

In Turkmenia however, the first meetings of the zhensovet were held in the spring and summer of 1959. The following year, in February 1960, the Turkmenian Party Central Committee organised a republic meeting of women from which groups of volunteer activists were sent to the regions to work in conjunction with the party organisations, the *Komsomol* and the trades unions to set up not zhensovety but 'Commissions for Work Amongst Young Girls' (Karryeva, 1969, p.16). One party activist suggested the introduction of 'family cafes' as a means of enabling women to participate more in public life (Shitarev, 1959, p.31). In Alapsevsk *raion (Sverdlovskaya oblast')*, reference is made by a town party secretary to their unsuccessful attempts to work with housewives,

Then in February 1957 the *gorkom* organised a zhensovet in one of the town's enterprises. By the following year there were thirteen zhensovety in the town involving 750 women. For the second year now, housewives have been attracted to social life. The party *gorkom* had previously tried to find a way of involving housewives in social work but with little result. We took too little account of their isolation, of the fact that they are tied up with domestic chores. We forgot that work with any one group can only be successful with the support of people in that group. We did better when the zhensovety were organised (Kazantseva, 1958, p.46)

Tallya (1971, p.220) affirms that a number of different approaches were tried at the time.

Both the confusion and the differing approaches in implementing the policy contributed to the description of the zhensovety as 'ad hoc'. After this initial period though, there was a general tendency towards uniformity. Party members increasingly spoke in favour of the zhensovety in preference to other forms of work amongst women, for example, 'the zhensovety are able to, and must, play an important role' *(Partiinaya Zhizn,* No. 11, 1959, p.24). A party official in the agitprop department of the Leningrad *obkom* for example, in emphasising the importance of the differentiated approach, links it with the zhensovety. 'It is this very differentiation of aproach to women workers and *kolhozniks* which is put into effect by the zhensovety formed in the Smolsky *raion* of Leningrad, . . . They organise socialist competitions, form women's clubs, involve housewives in public life (Sapozhnikov, 1962, p.452).

Various means were used to popularise the zhensovety. The same official suggested that activists should start collectives in residential areas using the home of an activist as a base. In some regions the party itself was active in setting up zhensovety.

> The buro of the *obkom* approved the initiative of the Barishtsev zhensovet and decided to make their experience accessible to other regions. About 300 activists were soon sent from Ul'yanovsk into the villages and towns to hold meetings with *kolhozniks* and workers in the *sovkhozes* and industrial enterprises. Everywhere one question was discussed: 'The role of women in fulfilling the adoption of the 1960 socialist responsibilities'. Following discussion, zhensovety were set up. Almost 95,000 took part in these meetings. (Polegeshko, 1961, p.6)

In some cases, the zhensovety were set up on the initiative of local women rather than the party organisation. In Alapaevsk (Urals) for example, the local party is reported as 'initiating' a zhensovet, but this was after M. Gurtovnik, a veteran party member, former member of the zhenotdel, had herself gathered together a number of housewives and pensioners in 1957, because in her words, they were 'discontented'. The women organised 'subbotniks' (voluntary work days) to clean up the town. The *gorkom* considered that Gurtovnik's efforts were 'unsystematic' and decided to hold a town meeting of women. At this meeting (17 March 1957), seventeen women were elected to form a zhensovet, with Gurtovnik as the

Chair. This zhensovet then went on to set up others at various work places (Gurtovnik, in Buzonova and Popova eds., 1963, pp.475-6). The zhensovet in Miass (Chelyabinsk) also has a 'spontaneous' beginning. In February, 1959

After the factory's pre-plan meetings there was an evening of leisure . . . this had been organised on the initiative of the women, and it turned out to be a first rate evening. It was then that the trades union committee of the 'mass cultural section' got the idea of forming a zhensovet. (Cheremnykh ed., 1964, p.31)

Whilst none of these examples provide firm evidence of local initiative and spontaneous action by women themselves, they do show that the lack of a central directive provided space for diversity, and help explain how the zhensovety came to be associated with 'ad hoc', spontaneous characteristics. The restraints on these features though serve to qualify any support they might provide for a collective female consciousness. Despite their 'ad hoc' appearance, the growth of the zhensovety arose primarily not from women's demands but as a result of CPSU policy. Nor are diversity and spontaneity always presented as positive features. Throughout their existence, discussion on how to strengthen the zhensovety has been linked to making them more uniform by centralising their organisation. This will be examined in terms of zhensovety relationship with the CPSU. The following chapter will discuss what 'initiative' and 'independence' mean in terms of zhensovety structure and organisation.

NOTES

1. Translation of 'obshchestvenie' varies with different sources. Included are 'voluntary organisations', 'social self help' organisations, and 'interest groups'. Madeline Drake's use of 'social' in inverted commas is adopted here to remind the reader that they are peculiarly Soviet institutions (Drake in Brine, Perrie, Sutton eds., 1980, p.144).
2. The *Spravochnik Sekretariya Pervichnoi Partiinoi Organizatsii* (1980, p.314), lists 'social' organisations as follows: zhenskie sovety; house and street committees; guardian councils; parents' committees; comrades' courts; societies, clubs and libraries; and organs of public control.

Friedgut (1979, p.243) divides 'social' organisations into three main groups: (a) control of public order; (b) mobilisation for state plans and participation in political activity; (c) voluntary support and service, either to supplement administration or represent citizens. Any one group may have a combination of these functions.

3. See also V. N. Konukhovskii and N. M. Ovlayannikov, '21ii Kongress KPSS i politicheskoi zadachakh partii v period obushchestvleniya semiletnovo plana', *Znanie Vsesoyuznoe Obshchestvo* No. 23 (1960) pp.17-28.

4. This theme was the subject of numerous articles and speeches at this time. See for example, Shitarev (1959) p.25.

5. V. I. Vasil'ev, *Sovetskoe Stroitel'stvo* (Moscow, 1967) quoted in Friedgut (1979) p.45.

6. During the Khrushchev period discussion showed there was some disagreement about such a definition. See for example, V. I. Razin, *Politicheskaya Organizatsia Obshchestva* (Moscow, 1967), pp.156-7 who disparagingly asserts that 'any socially useful work performed by the masses is seen as self government. Thus mobilisation to clean up the neighbourhood qualifies as participation'. Quoted in Friedgut (1979), pp.25-6.

7. Our starting point has been adequately expressed by Elizabeth Boulding (1977, p.224): 'The ideology of participation means that all mechanisms which assist individuals in making decisions that shape their lives get serious attention'.

There has been increasing recognition amongst scholars of the Soviet system who seek to explain its stability rather than predict its collapse, that an important role is played by citizen participation in the 'social' organisations. See for example, Bialer (1980) p.177.

8. For origins and explanation of this concept see Antonio Gramsci, 'State and Civil Society' in Hoare, Quintin, and Smith eds. (1971).

9. '. . . they (the 'social' organisations) put into practice the line of the CPSU for gradually converting the organs of state power in communist society for self government'. L. I. Brezhnev, *Stenograficheskie Otchet* (1962), p.348.

10. Yuri V. Andropov, report to the Central Committee, plenary session on 'Re-adoption of Decisions of State and Public Life' (5 June 1983) (trans. *CDSP* Vol. XXXV, No. 25, p.6).

11. *Spravochnik Sekretarya Pervichnoi Partiinoi Organizatsii* (1980), p.314. These figures do not represent an active membership. Dual membership occurs to a considerable extent. Women in the zhensovety for example, frequently participate also in other groups such as their trades union, parent committee and local soviet. Soviet authorities themselves disagree about the extent of active membership, see Friedgut (1979), p.244 and Bialer (1980, p.189).

12. On 11 March 1959, the Ukraine Central Committee adopted a key resolution on the 'differential approach'. A. Tolmachevi and G. Il'nitskaya eds. *Voprosy Ideologicheskie Raboty* (sbornik razhneishikh reshenie KPSS (1954-1961 gody), (Moscow, Politicheskaya

Literatury), p.132. Discussion of this resolution refers to the necessity of developing more varied forms of work to implement the decisions of the 21st Congress CPSU. The work of the agitational centres, [*agit punkts*] is criticised. A call is made for closer links with the masses and the Central Committee measures to introduce a 'differentiated approach' for political work amongst workers and sections of the population such as women. Mention is made of residential areas, and a list included of suitable forms of work such as formation of clubs, *agit punkts* and festivals. *Partiinaya Zhizn,* No. 6 (1959), pp.22-30.

13. The percentage of female delegates to party congresses notably increased, from 15.3 per cent (20th Congress) to 22.3 per cent (22nd Congress) C. Saikowski and L. Gruilow eds. (1962) p.119.
14. A resolution adopted on 9 January 1960, 'O zadachakh partiinoi propagandy v sovremennykh usloviyakh', also refers to women as a specific social group. It calls for attention to women, especially housewives, with more ideological education. Lectures and talks for women should increase and be at a higher political level. *KPSS v Resolutsiyakh i resheniakh* T.8 (Moscow, 1972) pp.37-58. This resolution, together with the one adopted on 11 March 1959 referred to above, appears frequently in sources on political work amongst women.
15. Z. Dakhimbabaeva (1958), pp.59-60 writes that in Uzbekistan, 'Lately special lectures . . . for women have been held, . . . One of the most important tasks of the CPSU, is the systematic and comprehensive work amongst women'. In her position as a secretary of the Uzbek Central Committee, Dakhimbabaeva criticises the poor efforts made to involve women in leadership positions at this time. She refers to the potential role of the zhensovety in improving political work amongst women and cites in this context the success of the 1st Uzbek Women's Congress.
16. This is illustrated for example by V. Kuriedov, secretary of Sverdlovsk *obkom* in an article in *Partiinaya Zhizn,* No. 9 (1959) pp.14-18. Commenting on the variety of activity taking place for women and youth, he highlights the zhensovety: 'Above all it is necessary to note the activity of the zhensovety'.
17. 'Yet practice fully contradicts this. The tasks of communist construction demand raising further the political and economic activity of women. In these conditions, the activists of the zhensovety take on even more significance. They are some of the most active organisations for involving women more fully in production and sociopolitical activity'. Tallya (1975), p.64.
18. '. . . the autonomous republics of Chuvashskaya, Mordovskaya and Mariiskaya began forming zhensovety between 1958-61'. Tallya (1971), p.221. Similarly in the Al'tai Krai, zhensovety 'were formed in almost all local places during 1958-61'. Brashnikova (1961), p.3. In Daghestan, the zhensovety were set up after the 21st Party Congress, El'darova (1963), p.68. See appendix 4 for table of zhensovety growth.
19. There have been two further growth periods for the zhensovety prior

to the 27th Congress CPSU. Sources refer to the late 1960s, which marked the Lenin centenary and the 50th anniversary of the Revolution. According to the staff member of *Rabotnitsa* interviewed in Moscow, the zhensovety 'mushroomed' during 1965-7. A third period of growth occurs in 1975, International Women's Year. Blekher (1979), p.22.

20. There is some discrepancy about the present existence of the zhensovety in Moscow and Leningrad. The staff member of *Rabotnitsa* said none now existed, as 'there was no need for them . . .'. Hough in Atkinson *et al.* (1978) p.362, writes: 'Moscow seems devoid of such organisations'. However, Zhvirble in Esieva and Shilova, eds. (1980), p.64 refers to zhensovety in Moscow. Although it is possible that her reference is actually to the trades union 'Commissions for Work Amongst Women' which, as was found from the interview with the Chair of a commission, are sometimes called zhensovety. According to a Moscow aquaintance, zhensovety exist in the micro regions of Moscow as knitting clubs and *'Klub Moskwich'* which appears on television, but these 'have nothing to do with the old zhensovety which exist outside Moscow' (1981).

21. *Bol'shaya Sovetskaya Entsiklopediya,* Vol. IX (1972, 3rd ed.), p.177, gives formation of the zhensovety as the end of the 1950s, beginning of the 1960s. Central Asia is cited as a region where the zhensovety are 'especially active'.

4 The Zhensovety: 'Independent' Organisations

The following three chapters will detail the activities of the zhensovety to explore why these social organisations have failed to provide greater access for women to political posts in formal politics. This will be approached in two ways: firstly by examining Soviet policy for consciousness raising, and secondly by investigating those features of the zhensovety which most closely resemble those of Western consciousness raising groups. We have argued earlier that if it can be established that the zhensovety operate with some autonomy this would be an important factor in the emergence of a collective female consciousness. This will be looked at in terms of zhensovety structure and organisation, and their relation to other organisations, in particular the CPSU.

ZHENSOVETY—STRUCTURE AND ORGANISATION

The features of the zhensovety as women-only groups, small, with members working on their own initiative in a collective, appear to echo consciousness raising groups in the West. The first point of difference, however, lies in their hierarchial structure. In most regions, local zhensovety are under the authority of other zhensovety at higher levels conforming to the pattern of other organisations. Like the CPSU, there is no zhensovet at republic level in the RSFSR. However, the zhensovety differ from other organisations in that they have no national co-ordinating body. This means 'There is no common structure and instructions for the zhensovety'

(Tallya, 1971, p.256). This is a further factor accounting for the diversity amongst zhensovety warranting a closer look at zhensovety infra-structure.

The exercise of authority by the higher level zhensovety varies from region to region. In some, the republic zhensovet has direct contact with local zhensovety as in Moldavia (*Krest'yanka,* No. 10, 1978, p.24). In Chuvash the republic zhensovet acts as co-ordinator (Tallya, 1975, p.62). In other regions, emphasis is placed on the 'directing' role of the republic zhensovet. More information is available about the activity of town and raion zhensovety with local groups. It can therefore be presumed that it is with these that the local zhensovety have the most contact. This relationship also varies. Some town and *raion* zhensovety understand their role as directing the work of the local groups. Local activists in Orlovskaya *oblast'*, for example, are presented with their tasks by the district zhensovet (Stoyankina, 1962, p.11). This is preceded by seminars to which *raion* and local activists are invited to 'exchange experiences'. They are then addressed by a party member or deputy on a political theme *(ibid.)*[1].

In some regions the raion zhensovety include representatives from the local groups, as for example in Barishskii *raion* (Ul'yanovsk) (Stoyankina, 1962, pp.6-7). This can be a two-way arrangement. In Edinetskii *raion* (Moldavia), the Chair of the *raion* zhensovet attends zhensovety in the *kolkhoz* (Rotar', 1976, p.22). In Sheduvskii *raion* (Lithuania) this contact is formalised by a member of the three *raion* zhensovety, each being attached to a local group for which she is responsible (Dobrodzeene, 1961, p.48). In other regions such as Tarakliskii (Moldavia) the role of the *raion* zhensovety is more remote, acting as a 'supervisor' and leaving the local zhensovety to formulate their own Plan of Work (Sibrayeva, 1961, p.44). Similarly in Chuvash, the *raion* zhensovety hold seminars for local chairwomen at which they present them with a general perspective for their work rather than detailed tasks (Tallya, 1975, pp.62-3). In turn, the *raion* zhensovet is described as a centre offering help and advice for local activists. A zhensovet Chair in Moldavia told a reporter, 'As activists, we regularly join up with the *raion* zhensovet to check our plans . . . and to share our experiences' (Rotar',

1976, p.22). Much of the zhensovety activity is replicated by each level (see Plans of Work, in appendix 3).

The variation in the relationship between zhensovety at different levels contributes to their apparently 'ad hoc' nature. The description of 'spontaneity' arises not only from the spasmodic formation of the zhensovety, but also from the time scale in setting up zhensovety at the different levels. In a number of regions local zhensovety existed prior to the higher bodies. One example is Oktyabrskii *raion* (Chelyabinsk) where the *raion* zhensovet was formed after the twenty-one local zhensovety. Its nineteen-member committee came into being for the express purpose of co-ordinating the work already taking place[2] (Vaganov in Kuznetsova ed., 1961, p.54). Nevertheless, the trend towards a hierarchial structure is clearly apparent. Even in cases where the local zhensovety existed prior to those at a higher level, they received retrospective 'approval'. Ardatovskii *raion* (Saransk) zhensovet for example when it was formed, 'approved' the 'initiative' of the women who had set up the local zhensovet some time earlier (Guseva in Dorozhkin ed. 1967, p.23). The description of the zhensovety as 'spontaneous' and 'ad hoc' is therefore explainable, although in reality it is evident that these features are of a most limited nature.

Zhensovety Membership

Although there are no official guidelines, the size of zhensovety groups follows the pattern discerned by Stoyankina (p.7) in her 1962 study of zhensovety in the RSFSR. The higher the level, the larger the committee. At republic level there can be as many as fifty; at district, thirty to fifty; *raion*, fifteen to twenty, and local as few as five upwards. The large groups mark a second point of departure from Western consciousness raising groups[3]. A third distinction is the committee. The zhensovety are committee-based, sometimes referred to as the *aktiv*, with the Chair as the most important position. Members are ostensibly elected by open ballot at public meetings or women's congresses[4]. According to Tallya (1975, p.62), the republic zhensovety are elected for a two-year period at congresses and the *oblast'* and *raion* zhensovety at conferences. The *gorod* zhensovet in Chelyabinsk for example was elected at a town conference (Kuznetsova ed., 1961, p.8). In practice though, the republic congresses are held less frequently[5]. Local zhensovety are encouraged to hold regular annual conferences (Moskvina, correspondence, 1980).

As far as can be discerned from the scant biographical information, the position of Chair is filled by a 'responsible' member of the community. These can be deputies, who appear to work in the zhensovety at a level commensurate with their responsibilities in the soviets. Thus in the republic zhensovety in Buryat ASSR (1961); Cheche-Ingushskaya ASSR (1980) and Moldavia (1981) the Chair was held by V. P. Boyanova, member of the Buryat Supreme Soviet; K. Dudurkaeva, member Cheche-Ingushskaya Supreme Soviet ('Order of Lenin', also Chair of the *oblast'* trades union committee, and *raikom*); and Anna Melnik, secretary to the presidium of the Supreme Soviet of Moldavia[6]. In the lower levels, the member in the position of Chair works in a 'responsible' occupation. Mention is made of teachers, doctors, librarians, a vet, director of a combine, a shop superintendent, and a senior book-keeper. The importance of the Chair is underlined by the seminars organised for women holding that post. This reinforces the hierarchial formation of the zhensovety.

At the same time, zhensovety structure presents some flexibility. Women do not have to be elected to take part in zhensovety organisation. Most zhensovety have sectors responsible for the different areas of their activities, to ensure their smooth functioning (Moskvina, correspondence). Attempts are made to widen the committee by drawing in other women, particularly specialists for the appropriate sectors. In the village of Veshkaimi (Ul'yanovskaya *oblast'*) all three sectors of the zhensovet were headed by non-elected women—a milkmaid; a teacher and a doctor. 'We did this consciously, in order to involve in the work of the zhensovet fresh strength and widen the *aktiv* still further' (Polegeshko, 1961, p.31). This writer considers the variety of activity and the flexibility of the sectors has contributed to the 'further growth in women's political activity' *(ibid.).* In most cases however, it is 'specialists' and existing members of other organisations who are asked to contribute their services to the zhensovety. The Barishskii *raion* (Ul'yanovskaya *oblast'*) zhensovet, consisting of representatives from *kolkhoz* and enterprises, had in addition assistance from almost forty specialists from hospitals, clubs and schools (Stoyankina, 1962). In the main, the zhensovety provide the means for women to perform their social duties rather than a place for women to gain social and political experience. On the other hand, the zhensovety cannot simply be dismissed as a carbon copy of other Soviet organisations responsible for women.

THE ZHENSOVETY AND 'INDEPENDENCE'

Barbara Wolfe Jancar suggests that one factor for what she sees as Soviet women's low political consciousness, is their lack of space to come together as women. This study suggests that the 'independent' nature of the zhensovety as women-only groups whose members work on their own 'initiative' presents a possible challenge to this assumption. This poses the question whether 'independence' and 'initiative' mean a level of autonomy enabling the zhensovety to be self-governing in both thought and action, or whether it refers to lack of an institutionalised formal relationship with other organisations. Does it provide space for innovatory concepts arising from women's shared experience, or is it an expression of individual activity within accepted guidelines? To answer this we will look at the relationship of the zhensovety to the CPSU and soviets and the political culture within which the zhensovety operate, the initiative of zhensovety activists and the role of party members in the zhensovety.

Zhensovety relationship to the CPSU and soviets

The most commonly used term to denote zhensovety relationship to other bodies is 'pri'. 'Pri' can be translated as 'attached' or 'under', which in English have quite different connotations. Perhaps in the case of the zhensovety it is best expressed by 'connected to'. This is a two-way relationship with the party and government organisations being responsible for the corresponding zhensovety in their locality and the zhensovety in turn being responsible to the appropriate committee.

There is some ambiguity about which organisations the zhensovety were responsible to initially. Sources refer variously to the CPSU, the soviets, and the trades unions. One early source stated that the zhensovety were being set up under party agencies and also under the management of the collective farms [*kolkhozes*], 'exclusively on a voluntary basis'[7]. Another source refers to the zhensovety working under the soviets (Strepuhov, 1965, p.15). The trend though was to bring the zhensovety under the auspices of the CPSU. By 1961, an article in *Partiinaya Zhizn* reports that 'the zhensovety are now being set up under *oblast'*, *gorod*, and *raion* party committees, to improve the organisation and co-ordination of their work'[8] (Shitarev, 1961). But this failed to be fully implemented. The same year as the article in *Partiinaya Zhizn*, the political committee of the local soviet in Novo-Mavakukon (Al'tai *Krai*), was organising under its auspices the initial meeting of a village zhensovet (Brashnikova, 1961, p.3). The only reference found of a formal relationship to another body is for the Buryat republic zhensovet, which is attached to the Buryat soviet, not the party. In a number of other regions, the zhensovety are reported to work more closely with their local soviets than with the party organisations[9]. Thus in practice the structural relation of the zhensovety to other organisations shows some diversity. This is further evident in how the relationship is manifest.

The CPSU relationship to the zhensovety is defined as one of 'guidance' or 'systematic help' (Myatieva, 1973, p.5). This can best be explored through the zhensovety 'Plan of Work', the detailed records of their tasks and activity. It will be borne in mind that the closer the relationship, the less likely is zhensovety potential for a collective female consciousness. Party involvement varies from region to region. In Odessa the zhensovet had their Plan of Work organised by the party (Polishchuk, 1964, p.3). In Moldavia, the Tarakliskii *raikom* 'constantly directs' zhensovety activities (Sibrayeva, 1961, p.44). Whereas during the same period in Chelyabinsk, the zhensovety drew up their own Plans of Work which were only afterwards presented to the party for approval (Zaitsev in

Kuznetsova ed., 1961, p.34). This variation and flexibility is underlined by contrast with the uniformity of the Commissions of Work Amongst Women and their relation to the trades unions committees (Biryukova, 1979).

This variation is also found in the day-to-day activity of the zhensovety. In some regions seminars are organised by the activists themselves, to which they then invite party officials, 'especially the secretary in charge of ideological work' (Tallya, 1975, p.63). In other regions party involvement is more direct. In the Stalino Donbass area of the Ukraine, quarterly meetings for zhensovety activists are organised by the party to inform them how to carry out party decisions. They cover such topics as 'The Central Committee January Plenum, both the overall plan and the specific tasks as they relate to the zhensovety' (Golovko in Koldova ed. 1961, p.384). However, even where the zhensovety do organise their own meetings and seminars, party officials play an active role. In Sverdlovsk for example, at a meeting organised on the 'initiative' of the zhensovet, the main speakers were the first secretary of the *raikom* on the subject of 'The Role of Women in Fulfilling the Seven Year Plan', and the second secretary speaking on 'International Women's Day and the Tasks of Women in Building Communism' (Stoyankina, 1962, p.14).

Whatever the diversity, the zhensovety are presented with the general guidelines for their work by party officials who address the women's congresses. At the 3rd Moldavian women's congress (1978), I. I. Bodul, first secretary of the Moldavian Central Committee, addressed the delegates on the tasks for women to fulfil their responsibility in implementing the decisions of the 25th Congress CPSU and the 14th Republic Congress (*Krest'yanka* No. 10, 1978, p.23). The active role of the party can be illustrated further by the agenda of a seminar for zhensovety activists held in Tarakliskii *raion* in February 1961.

The Central Committee January Plenum, both the overall plans, and the specific tasks as they relate to the raion zhensovet.
The 1980 Moscow Conference of Workers and Communist Parties.
The Struggle of women for peace and friendship among nations.
Preparations for the 8th March.
The preparation of children's establishments for the Spring and Summer.
(Sibrayeva, 1961, p.44)

The close relationship of the zhensovety to the party is further cemented by the attitude of the activists whose role is defined as 'helpers' to the CPSU. Stoyankina (p.14) claims that all who work in the zhensovety 'consider themselves as helpers of the party organisation'. Party seminars for zhensovety activists in Edinets *raion* (Moldavia) are 'to teach them how to help the party and soviet organisations' (Rotar', 1976, p.22). In return the activists are told how much the party appreciates their 'selfless work' (*Krest'yanka,* No. 10, 1978, p.23). Detail of this help is provided in a later chapter. Despite the lack of formalised structural relationship, the CPSU dominates the political culture in which the zhensovety operate. This is apparent from the content of zhensovety tasks, and the varying strands of connection between the party and zhensovety.

'Initiative' by Activists

'The zhensovety are set up by our public spirited women . . . where they work without remuneration and on their initiative' (*Krest'yanka,* No. 12, 1978, p.12). According to Ol'ga Tallya (1971, p.227), due to the 'initiative' of zhensovety activists, 'a number of measures exist for raising women's political consciousness'. Zhensovety activists in Tashkent are noted for their 'wide creative initiative' (Nasriddinova, 1964, p.170). Anna Paakhava, who heads the Lenskii *raion* zhensovet (Yakutia), works with the schools on her own 'initiative' (*5i S'ezd Zhenshchin Yakutii,* 1970). The activities resulting from such initiatives are already an accepted part of party and Soviet life. Meetings of solidarity with women abroad are an example: 'The party, soviets and trades union organisations greet this initiative, support it and give the necessary help' (*Krest'yanka,* No. 5, 1975, p.21). Initiative can also refer to more specific actions, such as in Khersonskaya *oblast'* where the zhensovet suggested a control post in a discussion on saving the harvest. 'The party supported the initiative and gave it direction' (*Krest'yanka,* No. 12, 1978, p.12).

Sometimes actions referred to as the initiative of a particular zhensovet have been recorded as taking place elsewhere. In Lithuania, a 'Flower competition' organised by the *raikom* for 'The best kept garden in honour of the 20th

Anniversary of Soviet Lithuania', is claimed to have had its origin in the initiative of the local zhensovet. But during this period there are a number of 'flower competitions' being organised by zhensovety. In other words, initiatives take place within accepted policies. Indeed, any initiatives which appear to differ are inevitably tailored to meet the norms of the political culture.

At first our zhensovety was bombarded with various requests, demanding much time, but there was not enough time to deal with them all . . . I will say openly to you comrades, we corrected this mistake. Now the conflict of which questions will be chosen is judged in a comradely way.

The speaker then gave a list of the chosen activities all following the general pattern of zhensovety activity at the time (*S'ezd Zhenshchin Buryatskoi ASSR Ii,* 1961, p.66).

The zhensovety task of mobilising women to implement the plans of party and government imposes a framework on their activity which serves to restrict local variation. It is also regretted that the zhensovety do not receive more direction from the party. So though 'initiative' is praised, in reality it is the implementation of existing party policies which is being applauded. Despite frequent laudatory remarks, initiative is also devalued. It is awarded low status because it comes from women. Tat'yana Sidirova conceded the usefulness of the zhensovety, but considered the range and variety of activities meant they lacked a definite purpose. For her the lack of systematic work undermined their serious intent: 'one cannot regard them as some sort of major serious school of a nationwide scope. This is just women's initiative finding expression under the guidance of party organisations' (Moscow, 1981). Such attitudes both contribute to sexism, and sum up the limited nature of initiative as used in the Soviet context. Initiative does not lead to activities outside the framework accepted as suitable for women. There thus seems little possibility of it serving to present an alternative to the existing male paradigm.

PARTY MEMBERS IN THE ZHENSOVETY

The relationship is consolidated still further by the zhensovety personnel. Whilst there is no obvious system of *nomenklatura*, it can be presumed that the vetting of committee members does take place. Party policy has been quite unequivocal about this since the early days of the zhensovety. 'The party in every way supports and develops in these organisations a spirit of initiative . . . and independent activity. The party puts its influence into these organisations through communists who are members of them' (Shitarev, 1959, p.34). Whilst this is the underlying principle, there is apparently no central directive regarding the number and position of party women in the zhensovety. Despite the lack of systematic data, sufficient can be gleaned to show that in this respect too the zhensovety vary from region to region. Sources such as Zhvirble (1980, p.164) which suggest that the majority of activists are communists are not supported by actual figures. In Moldavia for example, where 'thousands of communist women working in agriculture are zhensovety activists', it turns out that half the members of the republic zhensovet are non-party (*Krest'yanka*, No. 10, 1978, p.23). In Miass, only twelve of the fifty-five strong committee in 1961 were party members (Zel'dich in Kuznetsova ed., 1961, p.27). In Kazakh town zhensovet, seven of the seventeen-member committee were party members (Boleiko, 1980). This contrasts with the Zavod *raion* zhensovet (Saratov) where of the seventeen committee members, there were twelve party, one *Komsomol*, leaving only four members non-party (Belyaeva, 1962, p.18).

The party members often fill the posts of responsibility such as Chair. A number of sources refer to the zhensovety under the leadership of party members (*S'ezd Zhenshchin Uzbekistana 1i*, p.94). Tallya (1975, p.62) says that in Chuvash the *raion* and town zhensovety are 'headed by secretaries and other responsible workers of the *raikom* and *gorkom*'. G. B. Bobosadykova, for example, a secretary of the Tadzhik Central Committee, prior to that secretary of the Tadzhik *Komsomol*, was Chair of the Tadzhik republic zhensovet in 1980 (*Rabotnitsa*, No. 11, 1980, p.7). The same year, the Chair of the Tubinskoi ASSR republic zhensovet was T.Ch Norbu, a member of the party *oblast'* committee (*Krest'yanka,* No. 3, 1980, p.34). V. Mosunova, assistant Chair of the Mari ASSR republic zhensovet (1978), was also an instructor on the *obkom* (*Krest'yanka,* No. 3, 1978, p.14). Yet here again there appears to be no formal directive. Indeed, the suggestion that such posts are usually reserved for party members was strongly rejected by a staff member of *Rabotnitsa* interviewed in Moscow (1981). However, those not actually party members are likely to be 'responsible' people, who are 'politically educated' (Stoyankina, 1962, p.7). The non-party Chair of the Miass zhensovet was 'jokingly called the political commissar, and is the right hand of the secretary of the party committee' (Zel'dich, in Kuznetsova ed., 1961, p.28).

By this combination of party and non-party 'responsible' women, the CPSU doubly ensures that the zhensovety work within the context of party policy. In some regions this is cemented further. In the Altai, elections to the zhensovety are led by the party and the soviets. In Turkmenia in 1973, the party decided to attend to the staffing of the zhensovety as part of strengthening the work of the group (*Ashkhabad conference,* 1972, p.110). A factory zhensovet in Ashkhabad saw this put into effect: candidates were first discussed by the party and then by the zhensovety committee (Myatieva, 1973, p.7). The Buryat ASSR includes in the rules governing its zhensovety, one which stipulates that members are elected with the agreement and participation of the Buryat Soviet (*Zakony i Postavleni,* 1961).

It is clear that the characteristic of 'independence' ascribed the zhensovety does not entail autonomy from the CPSU. Nor is this likely to change in the near future. Recent discussion on the role of the zhensovety has centred on the need to strengthen further their relationship to the party. There are as many references to the ineffectiveness of the zhensovety as there are instances of praise. Low female status which led to the zhensovety in the 1950s finds echo in current reports thirty years later. The zhensovety have not done the job required of them. Activists are found inadequate. It has been argued that the zhensovety would be more effective if their work was more systematised, centralised, and if the party gave them more direction and had greater control. There is general acceptance that the quality of party leadership is an essential factor: 'The effectiveness of the zhensovety, as is well known, depends on the level of the Party and Soviet leadership' (Cheidene, 1980, p.117). Such ideas are not new and echo much of the debate around the zhenotdel.

Criticisms and proposals come from a variety of groups for different reasons. One group is the activists themselves. It is they who experience directly the lack of priority given women by the party. In the context of soviet society, the efficacy of organisations in terms of resources depends on the extent of party support, in other words of official recognition. Activists have accused the party of not attaching sufficient importance to their work. Belyaeva (1962, p.24) complains that the failure of the zhensovet to develop wide-scale activity in the town is due to the 'insufficient importance' given to this form of work by the party. In Suzemke (Buryansk), the zhensovet Chair decided that because the zhensovet 'did not always receive the respect it should' action had to be taken. This she did by addressing a plenary session of the *raikom* (Kuznetsova, 1962, p.7). Activists complain about infrequent and irregular seminars (*S'ezd Zhenshchin Uzbekistana, 1i*, p.94). Sibrayeva (1961, p.46) writes that the Tarakliskii *raikom* has only recently begun to pay attention to the zhensovety, and has done little to promote women to posts of responsibility in the *kolkhozes*. Given this attitude by party organisations, it is not surprising that activists complain of indifference on the part of trades unions and managers. 'Of course, not all zhensovety work is successful. There are still inadequacies. Social organisations, particularly the trades union committees, do not always respond in good time to zhensovety needs. This certainly reduces their efficiency' (Zaitsev in Kuznetsova ed., 1961, p.36). Another example comes from a zhensovet Chair who reports that the managers of a *kolkhoz* in Checheno-Ingushskaya 'have blushed more than once when called to account by the zhensovet for ignoring their requests' (*Krest'yanka*, No. 9, 1980, pp.26-7).

Female academics, concerned with the as yet unrealised potential of the zhensovety, are another source of criticism. It is the academics who have suggested that the zhensovety have a central co-ordinating body. Tallya (1971, p.156) suggested both this and a republic zhensovet for the RSFSR. Zhvirble (1980, p.180), who emphasises the importance of the party's responsibility, suggests that the zhensovety should become 'social commissions answerable to the party organisations'. The zhensovety would then presumably parallel the women's commissions attached to the soviets and trades unions. Cheidene (1980, p.117) reiterates the policy of 'differentiation'. The zhensovety would receive 'further substance and direction' if the party and soviets 'study more deeply the differential approach for work among women, pensioners and girls'. This is the background to Gorbachev's proposal that the zhensovety be integrated 'into a single system with the Soviet Women's Committee at its head' (*Soviet News*, 26 March 1986).

But strengthening party control has not been the only response. There have been calls for less party involvement, albeit mainly in the early period when 'participatory democracy' was much in vogue. One party theorist, for example, rejected the idea of the zhensovety being an 'appendage' of the party and called for 'flexibility and diversity' towards women (Shitarev, 1961). Some zhensovety activists have found their work benefitted from less association with the party. In Suzemke, educational work amongst women improved when organised by the zhensovet rather than the local party. The activists claimed that this was because their own approach was more 'delicate' (Kuznetsova, 1962, p.14). The main response, though, has undoubtedly been to extend party involvement. Two factors can be discerned in this. Firstly, that the zhensovety are not fully controlled by the party, and thus exercise a semblance of 'independence'. Secondly, the zhensovety, and by extension 'the woman question', have remained a low priority in the work of party organisations.

We have seen that there is some justification for the description of the zhensovety as 'ad hoc', spontaneous, independent women's organisations whose members work on their own initiative. The spasmodic emergence; the lack of an official blueprint and central co-ordinating body; the existence of local groups, sometimes set up by individual women prior to the higher structural levels to which they are responsible; the variation in size and party membership, and the wider involvement of non-elected women are all contributing factors. To this is added the lack of a formal structural relation to the CPSU or other organisation (with the exception of Buryat zhensovety and soviet), which allows the zhensovety to be called 'independent'. This is underlined by the very complaints about insufficient party involvement and control, which by default provide the zhensovety with more space. These characteristics however fall far short of creating the conditions supportive of the development of a collective female political consciousness. There are severe limitations. Despite their spontaneous, 'ad hoc' emergence, and lack of a formal directive, the zhensovety exist because of party policy: their origins did not emerge from women themselves. The very process of popularising the zhensovety favoured uniformity, with activists being encouraged to adopt activities and methods of work found successful. Initiative is contained within accepted frameworks of what constitutes 'women's work'. The purpose of the zhensovety to activate women and extend party influence presents them with *a priori* restraints. The actual relation to the CPSU illustrates how limited independence can be. It is the party norms in the political culture which provide the guidelines for zhensovety activity. The zhensovety thus appear to have little room in theory or practice to exert autonomy from the party. It is evident that despite the variation and the lack of a statutory relationship, they are expected to, and indeed do, identify with the policies and aims of the CPSU, both in general terms and with respect to women. There remains however, sufficient room for ambiguity to modify Jancar's assertion about the lack of space available to Soviet women.

NOTES

1. Seminars in Orlovskaya *oblast'* are organised as follows: activists from the zhensovety 'exchange experiences' and are then addressed on a political theme by a member of the local party or soviet. Officers of the *oblast'* zhensovet then inform them of their future tasks (Stoyankina, 1962, p.11).
2. Similarly the zhensovet in Ikurskaya *oblast'* was formed as late as 1976 to 'direct the work of all the region's zhensovety' (Cheidene, 1980, p.116). At the time this amounted to forty-three town and borough and 600 local zhensovety.
3. See Nancy McWilliams in Jaquette ed. (1974), p.64 who defines consciousness raising groups as being small groups of women.
4. 'The zhensovety today, like the delegates of the 1920s are voluntary organisations which elect women at a general meeting by a simple show of hands (*Otchizna*, 1981, p.4). What this can mean in practice was illustrated by the Chair of the trades union commission interviewed in Moscow. She herself had been pre-selected by the predominantly male trades union committee to attend a school in preparation for the planned 'Commission for Work Amongst Women'. Her unanimous election made sense, it was she who had received the training for the post. 'The chair of the mestkom [works trade union committee] suggested me as chair of the commission . . . . They recommended me because I'd already been working on this [ie attending the school], and because some of the women did not know me'.
5. The 1st Uzbekistan Women's Congress was held 7-8 March 1958, the second congress was three years later (16-17 May 1961). The 3rd Moldavian Women's Congress was held in 1978. The 4th Lithuanian Women's Congress was held in 1982, the same year as the 7th Komi Women's Congress. In many regions the first women's congresses were convened during the Khrushchev era in conjunction with the policy of differentiation and the introduction of the zhensovety. However, in Daghestan the 8th Women's Congress was held in 1961, the first having been in 1934.
6. *S'ezd Zhenshchin Buryatskoi ASSR Ii, Materialy S'ezda* (1961), p.7; *Krest'yanka*, No. 9 (1980), p.26; *Krest'yanka*. No. 10 (1978), pp.23-4; *Krest'yanka*, No. 2 (1981), pp.6-7.
7. In this respect the zhensovety are similar to other organisations; see Hill and Frank (1981), p.129.
8. Sources refer to party organisations, discussing the role of the zhensovety in the context of 'reanimation'. See for example the Communist Party of Daghestan: 'O rukovodstve partiinoi organiszatsiei sovkhoza "Kranyi Oktyabr" ' Dec. 1967 in Gasenbekova (1967), pp.16-17.
9. Belenkii and Rakhumov (1978), p.86 refer to the zhensovety as 'assisting' the work of the soviets. In Batetskii *raion* (Novgorodskaya *oblast'*), the soviets and their commissions work with the zhensovety on 'common areas of interest' (*Krest'yanka*, No. 1, 1980, p.28).

Much of zhensovety activity covers areas for which the soviets have responsibility, such as pre-school provision and environmental matters. Close association between the soviets and the zhensovety is unlikely to be contested by local party committees, as direct responsibility by them for the zhensovety would increase their work load. Especially as the close relationship between the soviets and the party organisations entails that the zhensovety would anyway be working under 'party guidance'.

5 The Zhensovety and the New Communist Woman

The politicisation of Soviet women is understood to rest on two main spheres of public activity: the economic and the political. It is the integration of these that will bring about the 'New Communist Woman'. The 'ideal type' for this new woman is a person who successfully encompasses the responsibilities of wife, mother, worker and citizen. Although the difficulties of this Herculean task are acknowledged, it is believed to be realisable, with the help and support of zhensovety (Khakhalov, *S'ezd Zhenshchin Uzbekistana*, 1961, p.51). The activities of the zhensovety therefore reflect this all-round Soviet person.

> The zhensovety . . . involve women workers in social activities, direct the moral education of the growing generation, struggle to overcome past traditions, help organise public services and facilities in populated areas, help the protection of nature, public control, work for the strict observance of the rules of labour protection, organise women's domestic life, control the work of public catering. (Cheidene 1980, pp.113-4)

Selection from this formidable list varies from group to group. Most zhensovety have sectors responsible for each area, but this is not institutionalised. One group in Tashkent for example, has nine sectors: production, agitprop, cultural and enlightenment, care of mother and child, nationalities, education, aetheism, cultural life and legal (Babadzhanova, 1971, p.110). A plan of work (see Appendix 3) shows how the general aims are interpreted. Generally these activities converge round two main concerns, the socio-political and the economic, as Tallya (1975, p.54) sums up, 'The zhensovety aim for the wide involvement of women in productive and social political life'.

ECONOMIC ACTIVITIES

Although the economic and the political activities are considered to be the twin prongs of consciousness raising, emphasis is placed on the economic. Ways are sought to raise women's productivity in the expressed belief that 'the basis of women's equality lies in socially productive work' (*ibid.* pp.51-2). For this reason Ol'ga Tallya considers the CPSU should strengthen the zhensovety so that they can increase women's working activity. Women's participation in paid employment introduces them to the public sphere. Raised consciousness, that is socialist commitment, is indicated by over-fulfilment of the plan. Thus when Soviet sources claim that the 'work of the zhensovety has led to the growth of consciousness of many hundreds of women' (Kuriedov, 1959, pp.17-18) it means that women are participating in the economy as 'active builders of communism'.

In considering the potential of zhensovety economic activity to politicise women in Soviet terms, we have to ask whether participation in the economy is to raise women's consciousness, or whether it is purely a justification for mobilising women around society's economic needs by using them as an additional source in a labour-intensive economy. Feiga Blekher believes the latter is the case.

> They are not organisations which are actively looking after the interest of women, and fighting to obtain a real fulfilment of the promises made to women by the CPSU and Soviet government. On the contrary, they are trying to get women to take on more and more obligations, to labour harder in the economy and to think less about themselves. (Blekher, 1979, p.22)

A different interpretation is provided by Richard Stites which will be considered later in the context of the zhensovety acting as a welfare agency for women. This section will consider the question in terms of zhensovety activity to mobilise women and raise women's status in the workplace.

The Zhensovety and Mobilisation

The mobilising role of the zhensovety has been to bring 'non-working' women into the productive process and, more frequently, to increase quality and volume of productive output (Tatarinova, 1958, p.68). Activity to encourage women to go out to work revealed that they were prevented by inadequate provision of child care. In one *kolkhoz* for example, labour shortage led the party secretary to advise the zhensovet to organise a meeting of all 'non-working' women. Two main reasons emerged for women not working: child care, the main one, and the wish to concentrate on personal lives, the other. Women who professed the latter were 'shamed' into entering the work force. The child-care problem was resolved by the zhensovet invoking assistance from grandmothers. Twenty women then started work, 'a whole brigade' (Stoyankina, 1962, p.17). Hence to enable one group of women to work, another group of women had to take over their maternal gender role. The Buryat zhensovet engaged in similar activity, gained the praise of the party speaker at their first women's congress: 'to the credit of the zhensovet, many former housewives are now participating in the working life of the *kolkhoz*' (*S'ezd Zhenshchin Buryatskoi ASSR, 1961*, p.54). Entry into the world of work had educational support. In the village of Staro Timoshko (Barishskii *raion*) in 1959, the inaugural meeting of the zhensovet was accompanied by an exhibition 'Women at Work'.

The increase in the proportion of women in paid work has been one of the major changes in the life of the zhensovety. Those not employed are mainly concentrated in Central Asia, where large families remain the norm. The main explanation, inadequate child care, has not changed over the years, but the proposals have. The emphasis is now on paid 'home work', part-time work and the shorter working day. This policy was introduced at the 25th Party Congress, and reiterated at the 26th, and by Gorbachev at the 27th Congress: 'In the 12th five year period we are planning to extend the practice of letting women work a shorter day or week, or to work at home' (*Soviet News*, 26 February 1986, p.85). In Tadzhikistan the zhensovety have been involved in its implementation. A questionnaire in 1980 organised by the republic zhensovet and sociologists showed 40 per cent of women in paid work, far below the national average. Large families of 7-10 children was one of the main explanations. Others were lack of suitable employment and lack of creche places due to 'failure to implement the plan'. Many women said they would 'willingly work at home'. Recommendations were made for the local provision of 'home work'. The ministry was asked by the Tadzhik Party Central Committee to detail plans. The Chair of the republic zhensovet concludes her report: 'I think the problem of working women is already being correctly resolved. One result [of the survey] is the 4,000 home workers . . .' (Bobosadykova, 1980, p.9).

In the main, the zhensovety concentrate on the second aspect of mobilisation, the quality and volume of output to meet the demands of the current economic plan. 'The role of the factory zhensovety is to mobilise all women workers for fulfilling the plan, to put life into the decisions of the 24th Congress' (Myatieva, 1973, p.5). In Rostovskaya *oblast'* following the 26th Party Congress (1981), zhensovety activists spoke to women on the tasks in front of them, particularly about raising production (Imamova, 1981, p.21). One of the main ways women are encouraged to improve output is by entering 'socialist competition'. In a factory in Chuvash ASSR for example, the zhensovet in conjunction with the trades union committee organised a course to raise women's qualifications and encourage participation in socialist competition. 'The result was 80 per cent of the women workers participating in the title "shock worker of communist work" ' (Tallya, 1971, p.233). Similar claims of success are made by a number of zhensovety[1]. In keeping with the practice of other Soviet organisations the zhensovety mark special events and party congresses by stepping up production. In Lithuania, International Women's Year (1975) was celebrated by the republic zhensovet with a call to fulfil the five-year plan (Dirzhinskaete, 1975a, p.28). The Rostovskaya *oblast'* zhensovet received awards from the district party and soviet committees for its success in encouraging 'socialist competition' to mark the party's 26th Congress (Imamova, 1981). Zhensovety activists are themselves expected to set a good example, as the Chair of a zhenovet reports, the activists 'spend every spare moment in the fields to carry out their responsibilities' (Kol'tsova, *Krest'yanka*, No. 12, 1980, p.22). 'Inventive and rationalising' work is another means used to improve the quality of work, as illustrated by the Berdsk Plan of Work (Cheidene, 1980, p.116).

Claims are made for zhensovety effectiveness in raising production. A. Egorova, assistant Chair of a regional zhensovet and secretary of the political committee of the regional soviet writes:

> Experience shows that when the zhensovety work with their full strength, and from the soul, there is proof in higher production and a fuller cultural life. Take for example, the *kolkhoz* . . . in Uzlovskii raion (Tul'skaya *oblast'*), this is a strong advanced kolkhoz. Not a little of the success belongs to the zhensovet of 15 women, headed by economist Bogacheva. There is no place where you will not find these female social workers. Their sharp eyes immediately notice anything out of order. (*Krest'yanka*, No. 4, 1977, p.2)

There is far less evidence of the zhensovety themselves having an input into these plans they mobilise for, but claims for such do exist. A delegate to the 5th Chuvash Women's Congress reported that at the Chuvash State Agricultural Experimental Station, the zhensovet participates in 'planning the budget, determining the Fund for Social Development, and its expenditure' (*Krest'yanka*, No. 11, 1978, p.22). Another source claims that in Lithuania the zhensovety takes part in local discussions of socio-economic plans which then 'find reflection' in state plans. (Purvanetskaiete, 1980, p.2)

The reports of zhensovety work indicate that mobilisation for production is undoubtedly the main motivation for much of their economic activity. In terms of raising gender awareness it can be construed as the antithesis to political consciousness raising. It means the zhensovety are activating women to meet the economic demands planned primarily by men. Given that takes place in a situation of continuing inequality in the division of labour, increased economic activity by women curtails the time available for political activity. However, though mobilisation predominates it is not the sole facet of zhensovety activity in the economy.

Raising Women's Status in the Workplace

Raising female qualifications is seen as part of furthering women's status as the 'New Communist Women'. As we have seen, this can be directly linked to increased output. But this is not the whole picture. Women predominate in the areas of production which are labour-intensive. This has contributed not only to the poor quality of women's lives, but also to their low status. In some regions, such as Mari ASSR, the zhensovety have seen the introduction of women to mechanised labour as one of their main roles (*Krest'yanka*, No. 3, 1978, pp.18-19). In regions like Daghestan, where there is little tradition of women in technical work, the zhensovety encourage young girls to enter professional and technical schools (Gasenbekova, 1979, p.14)[2]. In this work too the zhensovety claim some success. The full mechanisation of the *kolkhoz* 'Bolshevik', Val'kovskii raion (Khar'kovskaya *oblast'*) is reported as largely due to the work of the zhensovet and its Chair (Fomina, 1978, pp.18-19).

To help women raise their qualifications the zhensovety organised training schemes with the trades unions. In Sverdlovsk *raion* (Orlovskaya *oblast'*), the zhensovet encouraged women to join beginners' economic courses and attend seminars on practice in agriculture. Women who improved their qualifications as a result had their names up on the wall newspaper and announced on the local radio (Stoyankina, 1962, p.7).

Although there are fewer references to this form of activity than to mobilisation for increased production, it does show the latter is not the complete picture of zhensovety economic activity. This suggests that Blekher's assessment is too harsh, a suggestion that will be supported further by looking at the zhensovety as a form of pressure group in the workplace. If zhensovety claims of success in mobilising women could be substantiated, it would mean that in Soviet terms they have contributed to raising women's political consciousness. This is seen to be reinforced by their more overtly political activity.

POLITICAL ACTIVITY

Political activity by the zhensovety aimed at developing the 'New Communist Woman' includes both agitation and propaganda. Agitation is primarily associated with the mobilisation to meet economic plans on behalf of the CPSU. Soviet understanding of politicisation, though, is not limited to mobilisation. Agitation also takes place around activities more politically explicit. Propaganda is associated with political enlightenment on the theory and practice of the CPSU. In other words, politicisation is synonymous with acceptance or apparent acceptance of the politics of a male-dominated party. This sharply contrasts with Western feminism. To evaluate whether the zhensovety do politicise women in their own terms, we consider the activity which they define as political. This includes formal political education, practical activity, party membership, anti-religious propaganda and socio-political work.

Political enlightenment is primarily, although not exclusively, formal education in the theory and practice of the CPSU. Women are educated in the spirit of the 'high moral principles needed for the building of communism'. This, for example, was the aim of the Women's University initiated by the Zhdanov *raion* zhensovet (Moscow) on the theme 'The Communist Way of Life' (Stoyankina, 1962, p.7). Most sources refer to the zhensovety performing a political role, 'the zhensovety play a definite role . . . in the struggle for the communist education of women' (Petrova, 1970, p.135). The broad nature of what this entails is illustrated by the Declaration 'Addressed to all women' adopted at the close of the 2nd Uzbek Women's Congress (17 May 1961).

It is also important to carry out political education work amongst women daily, especially where they live. We need to vary the forms and methods of our work. We need to involve more women in political enlightenment, in the people's universities of culture and to strengthen anti-religious propaganda. Our duty, comrade activists, is to constantly help the party organisations educate all women in the spirit of high ideals. The main task of political work is the education of people by positive example. Education in the individual is a mark of communist character. We will struggle against backward attitudes to women.

According to zhensovety Reports of Work, political meetings for women are extensive in many regions. In 1960 for example, the Tarakliskii *raion* zhensovet (Moldavia), with the party and Society for Spreading Political and Scientific Knowledge, organised 367 lecturers, half of whom were women. During that year they gave 1,500 talks, 750 of them being to women only in the zhensovety. These included 200 on agricultural topics and 103 on medical themes (Sibrayeva, 1961, p.44)[3]. Themes ranged from those associated directly with mobilisation: 'The Role of Women in Fulfilling the Tasks Proposed at the 22nd Congress of the CPSU', to politically informative topics like 'Soviet Foreign Policy', and gender-specific themes like 'The Role of Women in Strengthening Peace on Earth' and 'The Soviet Women's Federation' (Zaripova, 1965, p.32). Political enlightment is primarily, although not exclusively, formal education. Despite the plea to 'vary the forms and methods', the main approach by the zhensovety to educate women politically, remains 'congresses, meetings, conferences and rallies' (Tallya, 1971, p.228). Such events usually consist of a 'political expert' handing out material to a passive audience. Questions may be asked, but there is seldom the format for a general discussion. The limitations recognised in the formal lecture have generally led to them being 'dressed up' by the inclusion of a social event or quiz. In Tarakliskii *raion* for example joint meetings of the zhensovet and *Komsomol* for young people take the form of a short lecture on a contemporary theme followed by entertainment, usually a performance by an amateur group, with a quiz or 'other activity which the young people can join in' (Sibrayeva, 1961, p.44). As in the Uzbek declaration, activists are critical of the formal lecture. N. A. Koval' (1961, p.14) the Chair of the Black Sea zhensovet, who emphasises political work with women[4], pointed out in the early 1960s that 'dry, jargonised lectures and talks, long and uninteresting meetings, only serve those who actually come.' Proposals to vary the form of educational work have been put into effect in some regions. Koval' talks of using every available opportunity to talk to women about their lives in general and the activities in particular. For her this is an important aspect of political activity (*ibid.*, p.16). This enterprising Black Sea zhensovet also used what are known as 'Oral Journals'. The idea is to make the presentation more lively than a formal lecture. Leading members of the zhensovety joined by other 'specialists', act out political events to their audience[5]. Another approach was to organise small group discussions. The Black Sea zhensovet began its political education programme on the 1st October each year with political study circles on current politics led by 'propagandists' from the Black Sea Fleet. These were attended by activists twice monthly (*ibid.*, pp.14-15). Despite these attempts to vary the form of political activity, Koval' remains critical:

It must be said however, that we do not consider our work to be fully satisfactory. There are still insufficient sailors' wives taking part in circles and political schools. The agitational work in the houses is weak and the zhensovet has a great deal to do in this area of work. (*ibid.*, p.18)

More satisfaction was expressed with the work of discussion groups which took place in women's homes in Chelyabinsk. In 1961 sixty housewives participated in various groups whose themes ranged from 'The Moscow Meetings of Communist Parties', to 'the Situation in the Congo'. Eighteen women took part in a discussion on current politics at House No. 14, whilst in House No. 1 women attended readings of Lenin (Kuznetsova ed., 1961, pp.4; 19). On the outskirts of Miass (Chelyabinskaya *oblast*'), the zhensovety ran twelve discussion groups, each of ten to fifteen people, in flats and 'red corners'. Each group included a member of the town zhensovet, the Chair of the local street committee and a deputy from the town soviet (*ibid.*, p.29). Although zhensovety activists have favoured an extension of such discussion circles and claim that in Chelyabinsk the party thought highly of this work, this form appears to be limited to the early 1960s.

A more common approach is to invite women to share the experience of others, especially war veterans and converts to atheism (Dirzhinskaiete, 1975, p.28). Another attempt to make political education less formal takes place around the 'agit punkts' and 'red corners'. These are rooms and areas set aside for political enlightenment at the place of work or residential area for which zhensovety activists frequently have responsibility. Newspapers, books and wall newspapers are available so that women who 'pop in' for a chat or information do so in a 'political' atmosphere. In the *kolkhoz* 'Lenina' Tarakliskii *raion,* the zhensovet has a 'kabinet' described as a 'light, airy room, well equipped for the use of women workers'. The walls are decorated with slogans and posters calling for implementation of the 1961 January plenum . . . . There is also a montage entitled, "Soviet Women, Active Builders of Communism" with a photo display of the best women workers' (Sibrayeva, 1961, pp.43-4). It is claimed that having such a study room has enlivened zhensovety political activity.

Women come there to read the newspapers and journals, listen to the radio, discuss activities of their brigade and get advice on questions of work, their family and their health, as well as help in form filling for pension claims and so on. Talks and lectures also take place here. (*ibid.*)

In Tubinskoi (ASSR) the zhensovet set up agitational departments in ten blocks of flats to which they invited 'specialists' to talk on a variety of topics 'most successfully' (*Krest'yanka,* No. 3, 1980). Similar work in Leningrad was claimed to be 'a step in raising women's political activity' (Sapozhnikov, 1962, p.453). Whilst the effectiveness of zhensovety political activity is questionable, it is evident that some activists have given thought on how to improve this area of work.

'Helpers' of the Party
The zhensovety are described as 'helpers' to the party. This could either contribute to women's politicisation, or be reducible to women carrying out duties on behalf of the CPSU. Gail Lapidus suggests, in her footnote on the zhensovety, that their occupation with 'local questions' of particular relevance to women 'enshrines "women's concerns" in Soviet political life as, in effect, a counterpart of "women's work" in the economy' (Lapidus, 1978, p.208). This analysis suggests that the zhensovety do take care of women's issues, but by so doing 'ghettoise' them without politicising women.

As helpers to the CPSU the zhensovety in the main carry out the tasks of mobilisation. But other tasks are also required of them. The zhensovety are involved in elections by helping at polling stations, organising meetings with candidates and ensuring that women 'carry out their duty as citizens' (Koval', 1961, p.18). In the early years the zhensovety were active in increasing newspaper readership, newspaper reading being thought to indicate political awareness. In the Stalinskii *raion* (Chelyabinsk), 100 women took part in getting every family to subscribe to a newspaper or journal (Kuznetsova ed., 1961, p.4). The zhensovety have also participated on particular issues, such as collecting aid for Vietnam in the 1960s. Since the 1970s they actively contributed to the Soviet Peace Fund. The Chair of the Liozonskii *raion* (Vitebskaya *oblast'*) zhensovet sending greetings in *Krest'yanka* to women shock workers, reported that in her region women contributed nearly 7,000 roubles to the fund in 1974 (*Krest'yanka*, No 7, 1975, p.22). In Estonia support for the Peace Fund was a factor in the award 'Best Zhensovet' 1975 (*Krest'yanka*, No. 5, 1975, p.21).

The political enlightenment activities of the zhensovety have no doubt enabled many Soviet women to be better informed both on specific issues and on general party policy. In this sense they do more than carry out women's concerns in the locality.

Party Membership
Much of zhensovety activity as helpers to the CPSU is the sort of social activity which is considered a necessary component of party membership. Experience in 'social' organisations has been a common background of many women in elite positions (Wolchik in Lovenduski and Hills ed., 1981, p.265). Insufficient biographical data on activists prevents an assessment of the role of the zhensovety in this respect. But it is evident that this notion of politicisation has not been translated into top political posts. This is most sharply expressed by the lack of women in the Ministry of Foreign Affairs, despite female association with 'peace activity'.

Few claims are made for a direct relationship between zhensovety activity and growth in party membership. Those that do exist fail to substantiate the claims made. Tallya cites the increase in female membership and posts in the Chuvash party as a consequence of zhensovety activity: growth of 3.1

per cent over a twelve-year period from 20.8 per cent in 1962 to 23.9 per cent in 1974, with twenty-four women in 1974 as regional and town secretaries, two of whom are first secretaries (Tallya, 1975, p.43). But it is impossible to ascertain to what extent the zhensovety were the effective factor in this development, although the republic zhensovet was concerned to improve the situation further by making the women's schools and universities more effective. The membership figures of Chuvash follow the general pattern of female party membership at the time. Another source claims that more women are in 'leading positions' thanks to zhensovety activity. By 'leading positions' though is meant up to district level in the party, deputies and 'the vanguard of production'. No data is provided (Belyaeva, 1962, p.24). It is more probable that the zhensovety contribute to the 'development of cadres' in the workplace. At the 2nd Congress of Uzbek Women, for example, the zhensovety were urged to 'prepare women systematically in the kolkhozes' (*S'ezd Zhenshchin Uzbekistana, 2oi*, p.69). The zhensovety prepare women for such posts, and in some cases remind managers and party officials of party policy. But this presents no real change in the political situation of women. There was no indication forthcoming in the interviews conducted in Moscow of how women's groups would contribute to the realisation of Brezhnev's calls for more women in executive posts. The Chair of the Commission for Work Amongst Women limited her response: 'the [trades union] commissions will help women get to such posts'.

The zhensovety thus appear to have had more success in raising women's political consciousness in the Soviet sense, than in introducing women into political careers. The extent of their achievements in political enlightenment can be considered further by reference to their work in what is termed 'anti-religious propaganda' or 'scientific atheism'.

'ANTI-RELIGIOUS' ACTIVITY

In Soviet Marxist thought religious belief denotes a low level of political consciousness. It is therefore incompatible with the ideal type 'New Communist Woman'. Religious influence amongst women was one factor which led to the formation of the zhensovety. Concern about this influence continues. Hence much of zhensovety propaganda work has focussed on 'scientific atheism', particularly in the Catholic regions of the Baltic, Muslim Central Asia, and areas in central Russia where the Russian orthodox church retains a strong foothold.

Zhensovety activity is again varied. In Lithuania, one of the first activities of the zhensovety in the 1960s was to organise an evening aimed specifically at housewives who 'know only one way of life, the Roman Catholic Church' under the rallying title, 'Let's All Get Together' (Dobrodzeene, 1961, p.48)[6]. This was followed up by Sunday evening talks on such themes 'To believe or not believe' (*ibid.*). In the Baptist regions of Sverdlovskaya *oblast'* and Chuvash ASSR, the zhensovety have held street meetings with former believers as speakers. One, for instance, joined female doctors for a meeting on atheism at the *kolkhoz* of 'The Red Army' in Chuvash to tell women about her conversion to atheism, whilst zhensovety activists had discussions with female members of Baptist sects (Stoyankina, 1962, p.15).

Some zhensovety have been active in the attempt to turn traditional religious festivals into socialist ritual. In the Urals for example, the zhensovet organised a 'Festival of the Streets' on the day of a religious holiday. A special evening for grandparents was included 'because of their influence on the younger generation' (Gurtovnik, in Buzonova and Popova ed., 1963, p.478). Similarly the Moldavian festival 'Mertzoi Shor' which celebrates the coming of spring has been incorporated into local zhensovet activity with the aim of making it' 'the exclusive care of women' (*Krest'yanka*, No. 7, 1976, p.22).

As with other areas of zhensovety work though, claims of success have to be tempered by the extent to which the perceived problem remains. Tallya (1975, p.17) admits that despite 'considerable success' religious belief is still strong amongst women. In 1976, the zhensovety took part in a commission in Uzgenskii *raion* (Oshskaya *oblast'*) Kirghizia, to seek ways to counteract the influence of religion (*Krest'yanka*, No. 8, 1976, p.10).

Due to differing concepts of what constitutes political awareness, it is debatable to what extent we from the West can assess the effect of zhensovety activity on political consciousness. Assessment is further hampered by the restraints on empirical investigation. With this constraint in mind, only a tentative assessment can be attempted.

The zhensovety appear to have had most success in mobilising women around the political and socio-economic decisions of the party and state. In Soviet terms this suggests that the level of women's political consciousness has indeed been raised. The extent to which this is so however, is open to conjecture. The effectiveness of the zhensovety as a mobilising agent has to be gauged in the context of low productivity and continuing economic problems. There are as many references to the ineffectiveness of the zhensovety as there are claims for their achievements. The material on the political activity was presented to see whether zhensovety activities politicise women; if so, whether this is in the Soviet sense of measuring political commitment by implementation of party policy or whether consciousness raising could lead to awareness of women as political. Despite the attempt to vary the form of political activity by some zhensovety, it takes place under the auspices of the CPSU and consists of themes within the acceptable political culture. The extent of success in Soviet terms can be gauged by the frequent criticism of political activity and the continuing religious belief amongst women, as well as the continuing low representation of women in the CPSU. There is no evidence that social activity in informal political organisations leads to growth in formal political institutions. However, the breadth of zhensovety activity modifies those assessments which either reduce the zhensovety to an economic mobilising machine, or carry out 'women's work' for the party. They do attempt to bring about the all-round character expected of the 'New Communist Woman'. It is their achievements which are severely limited. The following chapter will explore further the reason for this by looking at their social activities.

NOTES

1. In Staliino-Donbass three quarters of the women working in the town during the early 1960s 'work on collective and communist work in keeping with the aims of the zhensovet' (Prikhod'ko, in Koldova ed. 1961, p.9).
    In rural regions the 'Pasha Angel' award is given annually to the 'best woman tractor drivers and mechanics'. Details of these competitions are featured regularly in *Krest'yanka*. In Moldavia for example, a competition entitled 'The Romance of Work' was organised for young women under the slogan 'Girls subscribe and mechanize' (Vartik, *Krest'yanka*, No. 7, 1975). In Ikursk, the zhensovety have held competitions under the titles of 'Best at Your Profession' and 'Best Young Specialist'. For further information see 'Heirs of Pasha: woman and tractor in the USSR'. *Women and Eastern Europe Newsletter*, No. 5 (1982-3) pp.7-9.
2. In reality the position of working women puts such claims in context. A report of the 7th Komi Women's Congress (1982) attended by representatives of 652 zhensovety, refers to the sharp criticism of delegates about insufficiencies including low mechanisation for female manual workers (Rusakova, *Rabotnitsa* No. 1, 1982, p.12).
3. In one *raion* in Dushanbe in 1965 for example, 100 talks were given to women (Zaripova, 1965, p.32). In Stalinskii *raion* (Chelyabinsk), 300 lectures for women were organised in 1960, including some especially for grandmothers and young women (Kuznetsova ed., 1961, p.4).
4. Koval' (1961, p.14), writes further: 'They [women] must deepen their knowledge, learn the historical glory of the Communist Party' and Central Committee and government decisions.
5. Mollaeva (1978, p.60), claiming that this is a helpful form of 'enlightenment' work, describes what takes place. 'Large numbers always gather together in the auditorium. The speakers are women: old communists, party and social workers, scientists and artists. They have a wide range of material. The audience become better informed on questions of national and international politics, on contemporary literature and the arts, as well as receiving advice on child care and housework'.
6. Over 300 women attended, surprising the organisers. 'As it turned out, there was no need to entreat them to come'. The event included a talk on 'Women in Socialist Society', a concert by school children and an exhibition on cookery and needlework (Dobrodzeene, 1961, p.48).

6 The Zhensovety: The Conflict Between Consciousness Raising and Traditional Gender Roles

Research on women and political participation indicates that traditional gender responsibilities are incompatible with political activity (Kirkpatrick, 1974, p.221). Yet much of zhensovety 'social activity' includes tasks associated with such responsibilities. 'Social activity' also encompasses cultural work and attention to gender roles and the family. Zhensovety sources frequently locate social activities under the rubric of 'socio-political', believing they help raise political consciousness. This chapter considers whether the effect of zhensovety activity is to help or hinder that process.

SOCIO-POLITICAL ACTIVITY

Socio-political activity is interpreted broadly. How broad is clearly illustrated in the interview with 'Olya' the Chair of the trades union Commission for Work Amongst Women. In response to questions about the group's political activity, she cited the provision of a beauty consultant. This service had been organised so that 'women at work will always be beautiful, pleasant and always jolly. That's our task' (Moscow, 1981). This view of political activity is held widely. In Stoyankina's handbook on the zhensovety, she includes under 'Political Activity' the 'Universities for Women' which offer talks by various specialists, among them scientists, doctors, teachers, artists, chefs and models. According to the author the aim is to provide women students with, 'advice and counselling on health care, child education and housework'

(Stoyankina, 1962, pp.15-16). Stoyankina writes that 'in order to involve women in social life, it is necessary to present them with something interesting—such as lectures on child care'.

'Socio-political' activity therefore refers to a range of social activities, many of which are aspects of community education and social welfare. Of particular relevance here is the concentration of much of this activity to improve those very female skills associated with the sexual division of labour. A common feature of the zhensovety programmes are classes and 'circles' on aspects of home-making, with knitting, sewing, cooking and home management being particularly popular.

In the early years of the zhensovety some activists used these circles as an opportunity for 'enlightenment' by reading to the women whilst they sewed (*ibid.*). Some used them as a place for women to come together. In her report on the Black Sea zhensovety, Koval' says women favoured these classes because their husbands viewed them as legitimate pastimes and were therefore supportive. 'More than once, I heard a woman say. "When I am sewing at home, my husband helps me . . . prepares the dinner himself, looks after the children"; "My Volodya bought me some good thread" ' (Koval', 1961, pp.20-1). Certainly such classes were organised widely, the very first activity agreed by the Barishskii *raion* zhensovety for example, was a sewing circle (Polegeshko, 1961, p.30). In the Black Sea region it enabled the women to find work in the town's garment factory, with the support of the zhensovety Chair: 'Let the women engage in a useful activity, acquire a useful profession' (Koval', 1961, p.20).

The classes remain popular, but there is now less ambiguity about their role. When asked if the sewing classes organised by the trades union commission provided an opportunity for discussion, 'Olya' was adamant that there was no time for anything except to 'sew, sew, sew'. Whilst it did mean that husbands took responsibility for children the night of the class, that was of secondary importance. The classes were organised at the request of the women, since the poor availability of fashionable clothes encourages home dressmaking. The activity remains a legitimate pastime for women, indeed 'Olya' remarked that the government is at present propagandising for such classes. This was verified and also justified by Tat'yana Sidirova, the research specialist on women's affairs. She thought time spent on these traditional skills should be viewed positively. Firstly, it provides women with much needed relaxation, 'Knitting for example, is extremely relaxing and good for one's nervous system. Isn't it good that there should be a transition from strenuous work to this relaxing leisure activity?' Secondly, the end product is useful and an expression of female expertise.

Therefore today women see this as a kind of opportunity to distinguish themselves, to show their gifts and talent by doing embroidery, which is an art in its own right actually. So these are all hobbies. Before, women had to do these things to provide for their families, while now there is no such direct need for that—there is a developed light industry, one can buy all one needs. Now it is done to adorn everyday life. (Sidirova, interview, 1981)

It could be argued that this approach is positive in that it gives status to traditional female activities, but when placed in the context of other zhensovety activities, it can be seen as perpetuating existing gender roles.

Feminine Care for the Environment
One of these activities, also described as 'socio-political', is the responsibility awarded the zhensovety for 'public order'. This covers two main areas: the physical, which involves the appearance of their local environment, and the social, which concerns public disorder caused by 'drunkenness and hooliganism'. This responsibility for order in the public environment extends women's role in the private sphere to the public, without transforming the type of responsibilities[1]. This is clearly illustrated by a secretary of the Norlisk district party committee who praises the zhensovety for the 'motherly care' they take of their town, in keeping the streets and yards 'spick and span' (quoted in Bochkaryova and Lyubimova, 1969, p.216).

It is suggested that such activity arose from the 'spontaneous action' of women themselves. In the Urals, a group of women took the initiative of cleaning up their environment and tending local gardens. This led to the formation of a zhensovet (Gurtovnik, 1963, p.475). Such activity is considered worthy. Official encouragement, aided by exhibitions and competitions, made it widespread amongst the zhensovety[2]. Members plant trees, and decorate their local party offices with flowers (Rotar', 1976, p.22). Twenty zhensovety groups in Tuminsk *aimakh* (Buryat ASSR) between them planted 3,000 trees (*S'ezd Zhenshchin Buryatskoi ASSR 1ii*, p.90). In Edinets (Moldavia), the zhensovet initiative of decorating the party office with flowers was taken up by local school children (Rotar', 1976, p.22). In an article entitled 'Managers of their Fate' it is claimed that the activity of the zhensovety means village streets improve each year[3] (*Krest'yanka*, No. 1, 1978, p.11).

Some attention is directed toward the women's own homes. In the Ugenskii *raion* (Kirghizia) the zhensovet and local soviet spent two years educating women on how to keep their homes orderly. In what is described as a 'subtle and gentle approach' women were invited to each other's homes and encouraged to attend seminars on the theme, 'Every flat, every house: beautiful, comfortable and convenient' (*Krest'yanka*, No. 8, 1975). In Dzidzhinskii *raion* (Buryat ASSR) the approach was more direct. Members of the zhensovet toured houses and the local *kolkhoz* with a loudspeaker (*S'ezd Buryatskoi* . . ., p.53). Here we have 'home management' enacted on the streets.

Zhensovety responsibility for 'anti-social' behaviour is a further aspect of women's traditional role in the home now extended to the public sphere. Alcoholism with its adverse effect on the family is recognised as a major social problem. Drunks are dubbed 'disturbers of the peace' (Polegeshko, 1961, p.25). Women as 'maintainers of the peace' is a continuing aspect of zhensovety activity, with some describing it as the main one (*Krest'yanka*, No. 8, 1980, p.24). It has engendered varied responses by the zhensovety, from intervention in individual families to performing skits in the local community. In Val'kovsk *raion* (Karkovskaya *oblast'*), zhensovet activists found that they were having little effect on one man with a perpetual drink problem, so arranged for the local film studio to do a 'candid camera' sequence when he was 'under the influence'—with apparent success (Fomina, 1978, p.19). In Sheduva (Lithuania), the zhensovet publicly staged a 'mock trial' to portray 'the evils of drink', the judge, accused and witnesses all enacted by local people (Dobrodzeene, 1961, p.48). As with the attempt to undermine religion, the zhensovety have tried to establish new folk traditions. One zhensovet, for example, claims to have initiated a new holiday to mark conscripts' entry into the army to combat the drunkenness that dogged new recruits. 'At a general meeting we decided that activists should organise the events to celebrate new conscripts . . . this would take the form of a non-alcoholic holiday' (Fomina, 1978, p.19). The holiday became a regular event.

One of the more recent features of the drink problem has been its increase amongst women. As letters to *Rabotnitsa* and *Krest'yanka* show, help is forthcoming from the zhensovety. In one such letter, a zhensovet activist writes about a father who, concerned about the effect of his wife's drinking on their children, approached the group, having received no assistance from the local soviet. The zhensovet organised child care and treatment for the mother (*Krest'yanka*, No. 9, 1980, p.24).

The zhensovety claim to have had considerable success in this area of their work. In Barishskii *raion* (Ul'yanovsk), it is claimed that drunks are more afraid of being called up before the zhensovet than before the local party committee[4] (Polegeshko, 1961, p.26). The continuing problem of alcoholism, and in particular its increase amongst women, put such claims in perspective.

This form of activity reinforces traditional characteristics associated with women. Taken in conjunction with the other activities which foster female gender roles, there is little to suggest that women's political status will be enhanced, or their consciousness raised, by the 'socio-political' work of the zhensovety. One area of activity which could provide an antidote though is what is termed as 'cultural activity'.

CULTURAL ACTIVITY

Cultural work covers two main areas: leisure and cultural 'enlightenment'. This has the explicit aim of raising women's cultural level. As Soviet sources include cultural level as a factor for women's lower political participation, this area is especially pertinent to discussion of political consciousness.

In the attempt to widen women's cultural experiences, the zhensovety arrange group visits to the cinema, hold literary readings and press for increased library provision. Activities are frequently presented as a 'thematic evening'. A range of activities takes place around a chosen topic. Many of these cater for traditional gender roles, such as 'The Young Housewives' evening organised in Stalino *oblast*' (Prikhod'ko, in Koldova ed., 1961, p.11). A detailed report on activity around the theme 'Let's Talk About Family Activities' from Koval' (1961, p.10), Chair of the Black Sea zhensovet, illustrates this apparently contradictory nature of cultural activity. Preparation is very thorough: 'we work on a decorative, well-presented invitation ticket printed in the form of a special handbook, and presented to each woman on entering the Palace of Culture.' The handbook contains various items considered useful such as 'advice on housework'; 'how to encourage children to be tidy'; 'recipes for tasty dishes'. The women arrive 'festively dressed in a festive mood'. The invitation included the following verse:

> It must be hard to be a woman,
> To stand equal with a man
> By the engines roaring madly,
> To drive vehicles across the virgin land.
> And to give pleasure with a promised story,
> And to check the exercise books of your son,
> And to always remain womanly
> Loving, good and beautiful.

The evening included a variety of events: sessions on 'the high morality of the Soviet person', 'The Soviet family', and what are described as 'games for young couples'.

People spent a long time looking at the satirical wallpaper which depicted caricatures of teddy boys, drunks and those who destroy discipline. Much interest was shown in the preparation of a special recipe, whilst in the foyer, a group of women listened to advice on how to decorate a festive table . . . Much interest was shown in the competition for the best pie. Yes, and it's understandable, after all such contests are not that usual. There was also a successful exhibition of evening dresses organised by technicum students. The concert was on the theme of 'Love and Friendship'. The sailors' wives learnt not a little that was useful to them that evening.

Although the theme for the evening was the family it appears that little attempt was made to introduce change in the division of labour; on the contrary, most activities served to reinforce existing gender roles. As such it is hard to see how it could contribute to female politicisation. What it does show is that the zhensovety aim to improve the quality of women's lives. Koval' herself puts the thematic evening in the context of how her zhensovet has 'thought a great deal on how women's leisure time can be more serious, how their cultural and ideological levels can be improved and how women can be involved in the collective'. As seen earlier, Koval' is critical of much of their work. Black Sea zhensovet members frequently discuss, 'even argue', about the forms and method of their work. They try to avoid carrying out 'measures', 'for even the word is somewhat boring', instead have 'heart to heart get-togethers which do teach something . . .' (*ibid.*, p.22). This is what Koval' felt the family evening achieved.

Other zhensovety encourage women to join leisure circles. In Lizonskii *raion* (Belorussia), zhensovet members organised a choir for fifty-two kolkhoz workers, earning them the thanks of the local party committee for good 'mass cultural work' (*Krest'yanka*, No. 7, 1975, p.22). In Uzgenskii *raion* (Oshskaya *oblast'*, Kirghizia), the zhensovet, arguing that 'there is no culture without books', adding, 'and they are needed especially where there are young children', strove to provide every block of flats with its own library (*Krest'yanka*, No. 8, 1976, p.10). The enterprising Black Sea zhensovet set up its own library (Koval', 1961, p.17). In the 1960s a number of zhensovety held 'Readers conferences', often held in the workplace. Local librarians, as for example in Orlovsk and Ul'yanovsk (RSFSR), introduced a novel such as Sholokhov's 'Don' trilogy and then led discussion (Stoyankina, 1962, p.27). Others, such as the Chair of the Suzemke zhensovet (Bryansk) a librarian, read aloud to women in the *kolkhozes* (Kuznetsova, 1962, p.13).

It is probable that many women have benefitted from these

activities with other women. Time studies show though that women continue to have less time available than men for leisure activity.[5] The example of the thematic evening illustrates the limitations of the 'new' image presented to Soviet women. Certainly when taken in conjunction with another area of zhensovet activity, their work with children, the cultural activity is not an adequate antidote to the activities which support gender roles.

ACTIVITY WITH CHILDREN

Zhensovety activity with children is described as the 'closest and dearest' work of the zhensovety (Sibrayeva, 1961, p.45). It entails paying practical attention to child-care provision, child welfare and education. As child care in particular is a major worry for working mothers, zhensovety attention to it does not of itself necessarily reinforce gender roles. Indeed, much of their activity entails pressing for better facilities. Zhensovety activists though also act as 'watchdogs', supervising school meals and children's institutions. These welfare and educational aspects of zhensovety work with children contribute to its designation as 'women's work'.

Child Welfare
Women with children are faced with the dilemma of how to perform adequately their two roles: worker and mother. This is certainly recognised by zhensovety activists. In the words of one, 'The zhensovety does not forget the other side of their activities: to enable woman to work fully, in a good mood, she must be free from worry about her children and her family' (*Krest'yanka*, No. 4, 1977, p.20). What this means in practice is that zhensovety members themselves 'visit the nursery time and again', thus continuing the long association of women's responsibility for children. It is specified as an area of activity in zhensovety 'Plans of Work' as for example in the Berdsk (Novosibirsk) zhensovet (1978-9), as 'help to families with young children' (Cheidene, 1980, p.114).

Practical assistance is given to individual families, especially single and 'heroine' mothers. Although 'heroine' mothers are feted in the USSR, there is poor provision for their extra needs. In one Moldavian village for instance, the zhensovet organised transport for the children of a single parent and ensured she received the benefits to which she was entitled (*Krest'yanka*, No. 10, 1978, p.24). The Chair of another zhensovet keeps track of the thirty-six heroine mothers working in a local factory, making sure their children have places in pioneer camp (Rusakova *et al.*, 1979, p.6). Clubs are organised for heroine mothers (*Krest'yanka*, No. 10, 1978, p.24).

In the far northern autonomous republic of Komi, zhensovet activists are responsible for children in boarding school, acting as 'substitute mothers'. It is their job to see the children get a varied diet, are adequately clothed, and that 'even the smallest feels confident despite being far from their parents . . . with the Spring and the White Nights, and the children skating, the members of the zhensovet are on duty around the clock.' At the end of term they make the children's travel arrangements, 'even going with them part way' (Chuprova, 1981, p.10). In Ul'yanovsk, the wall paper 'Alga' reports zhensovet activists making clothes for children of large families, caring for the children of women in hospital, and helping during the school holidays (Stoyankina, 1962, p.24). Zhensovety activists therefore take on clearly defined areas of 'women's work'. This is underlined by their 'watch-dog' role in other children's institutions. In the Urals activists check on hygiene in schools and nurseries. In Alpaevsk this was in response to parents who reported dirty kitchens in Kindergarten number 14 (Gurtovnik, 1963, p.346). In Neivo-Shartansk activists took the laundry home to wash themselves (*ibid.*, p.477). In other areas local zhensovety are responsible for children's meals (*Otchizna*, March 1981, p.5). A reporter visiting a kolkhoz zhensovet in Moldavia found them discussing arrangements for the 'Day in the Defence of Children'. The Chairwoman pointed out that although the trades union and management provide the finance, it's the women who do all the organising—buying presents, providing the refreshments—just as it was they who organised the local kindergarten. Responsibility for children during school holidays has entailed toddlers' rooms, circles and clubs;

children's playgrounds (Kotelenetz, 1977, p.28), and a regional music school (*Krest'yanka*, No. 7, 1975, p.22).

Zhensovety activists take on the trivia associated with the lives of women as wives and mothers. One source actually states that they do not consider any matter too trivial for them (Vartik, 1975, p.7). Much of this work parallels that of local soviets. What the zhensovety do is perform those tasks identified as women's work.

Child Guidance
Zhensovety involvement with school children is an aspect of their 'social' responsibility to the community. Activists check on the child's moral and physical health both in the home and at school. They are also responsible for helping parents socialise their children as good Soviet citizens. This requires organising talks and lectures on child rearing, being involved in the child's school progress, and participating in school 'Open Days', parent committees, and consultation with teaching staff (*Otchizna*, 1981, p.5).

Poor progress at school is considered to indicate potential 'anti-social' attitudes. Zhensovety activists are therefore required to be aware of such signs. In the town of Cherpovtsa (RSFSR) the zhensovet Chair has a list of all local school children and a record of their school marks. If these are poor, the child's parents are invited to discuss them with the zhensovet. The 'Child Sector' members then give attention to the child as long as necessary (Stoyankina, 1962, p.23). This activity can mean considerable commitment and personal involvement by zhensovety activists. According to Stoyankina, some open their homes to school children and young people requiring guidance. She cites the activist, Alexandra Ivanovna Busheva, member of the Verkh Isetkom *raion* (Sverdlovsk), as a case in point, who had to deal with Tamara, 'a difficult pupil from class 5, school No. 73'. She met the child from school regularly, accompanied her to the children's club, sometimes took her home with her. She helped Tamara with her lessons, having first discussed the work with the child's teacher. She could eventually report that Tamara's marks had improved and she had joined the Pioneers (*ibid.*, pp.21-2).

The zhensovety continue to have responsibility for the

moral well-being of the young after they have left school. One report says, 'We deal with the problem of parasitism. The zhensovet understands the mood of young people . . . we give advice and carry out educational work . . .' (Vartik, 1975). In this case the zhensovet prepared for 'Occupations Day'. It meant every child in the leavers class who chose to work in agriculture was introduced to an experienced worker.

They talk not only about their work, but also about their studies, about life, the correct way to behave, style of dress . . . In these discussions our women try to establish close contact with their charges and influence their behaviour, their patriotism, their ideas and aesthetic education. (*ibid.*)

By being directly responsible themselves for what is perceived as women's work, zhensovety activists perpetuate gender roles. This reinforcement of women's maternal role contradicts Soviet theory which claims to recognise that women will lack full equality whilst the responsibility for children and the home remains with them. Some activity does help individual women. This could be construed as 'sisterly support' and there are indications, considered in the following chapter, to suggest that individual activists see it as such. Alternatively the zhensovety can be seen as a voluntary welfare service. In this respect activists are not only working within official guidelines, they are also continuing a traditional female role. The attempt to justify zhensovety involvement by giving it socio-political status does not undermine this. The ideal type 'New Communist Woman' is clearly one who is expected to work within traditional gender expectations whilst encompassing new ones.

THE ZHENSOVETY AND MALE ROLES

Reference to male roles within the family does feature in zhensovety reports, but marginally. Here we are concerned with determining the extent to which the transformation of gender roles is raised. Activists who do refer explicitly to the relationship between female equality and the male role, do so in the context of Lenin's maxim that 'much of the emancipation of women is concerned with the education of men', and the stultifying effect of housework. They point out that insufficient progress has yet been made to assist women with such tasks and this hampers their emergence as 'Active Builders of Communism' (Polegeshko, 1961, p.32). But although activists raise the issue sharply, their panacea is additional support for women rather than changing male roles.

However, there are some examples of zhensovety attempts to re-educate men. In an interview published in *Rabotnitsa* (No. 11, 1980, p.9), Guldzhahon Bobosadykova, secretary of the Central Committee of the Tadzhik Party and Chair of the republic zhensovet, reminding readers that Lenin considered female emancipation depends much on the education of men, reports that in Frunze *raikom* (Dushanbe) male candidates to the CPSU are required to answer: ' "Who is your wife? What is her profession; is she a Komsomol member; does she work? Do you help in the house, with your children's upbringing and education?" '

Activity on male roles ranges from general education to dealing with individual family problems. Some zhensovety have held events specifically on the 'father role', as for example in Chuvash, in this case at the instigation of the party committee (Tallya, 1975, p.55). Films on parenting with such titles as 'Father or Mother' have been shown (Belyaeva, 1962, p.20)[6]. In the Ukraine an evening on the theme 'The Beauty of Human Relationships' turned out to be an 'active discussion' on male and female public activity and the 'role of the family in building communism' (Koldova ed., 1961, pp.50-2). The reports are not sufficiently detailed to enable assessment of the content of these sessions.

The zhensovety intervene when individual male behaviour prevents wives from working, furthering their qualifications or taking part in social activities. Such behaviour is seen as 'backward' and 'feudal' and is frequently reported in Muslim regions. At a conference for social workers in Ashkhabad (1970), one delegate referred to the 'old view of women' which continues to 'restrict women to the family, caring for children, and leaves them at home to prepare for their husbands' (*Osvobozhdennaya Sovetskovo Vostoka*, 1972, p.99). In Turkmensk such attitudes led to direct intervention by the zhensovet. The husband of a worker in a sewing factory, mother of four children, was preventing her from taking part in 'socially useful work'. The zhensovet activist found that the husband was not a 'bad person'—'He was a good worker in his own way, loved his wife and children, but he adhered to the traditional belief that a wife was no more than an ornament in her own home'. Intervention by the zhensovet meant that the woman 'over fulfills her shift tasks and studies political theory for beginners at evening class'. At the *kolkhoz* 'Gigant' (Bogadakhiskii *raion*) husbands had forbidden their wives to attend the zhensovet. The zhensovet 'severely condemned' the husbands with the result that 'all of them, together with their wives, regularly attended the meetings and took part in social events' (Polegeshko, 1961, pp.30-1)[7].

Whilst it is evident that the question of male roles receives some attention, none of this begins to transform the sexual division of labour. Zhensovety intervention raises the question of gender roles, but this remains within the context of extending women's roles rather than radically changing men's. The intention appears limited to raising cultural attitudes to European norms.

THE ZHENSOVETY AND THE SOVIET FAMILY

Zhensovety activity on parenting, re-education of men, and their work with children and adolescents, takes place within the context of the Soviet concept of the family. The family as the 'cell' of society, is considered functional to its orderly well-being (Sedugin, 1973, p.6)[8]. It is evident from zhensovety activity that they are transmitters of this familial ideology. In his report to the 27th Congress, Gorbachev spoke of the need for further consolidating the family, and highlighted the role of 'social' organisations in this process. 'We have to structure the practical work of governmental bodies and mass organisations so that it would in every possible way help to consolidate the family and its foundations' (trans. *Soviet News*, 26 February 1986, p.85). Zhensovety support for the family takes three main forms: educational lectures and talks, welfare work on family matters, and focus on women's maternal role in the rearing of future Soviet citizens.

The educational work on the family is referred to by a number of zhensovety. The zhensovet in Edinets *raion* (Moldavia) have held seminars for activists specifically on their role in strengthening the Soviet family (Rotar', 1976, p.22). The republic zhensovet organised a seminar on the theme, 'How to create a strong united family and the women's role in this' (Belyaeva, 1962, p.19; *Krest'yanka*, No. 10,1978, pp.23-4). The zhensovety are also active in organising 'new socialist traditions' with celebratory festivals such as the 'Festival of Young Families' (*Krest'yanka*, No. 1, 1980, p.28). The zhensovety are likewise responsible for civic functions associated with the family. In some regions, as in Kokchkavskii *raion* (Kazakhstan), they perform the registration of births and marriages (*Krest'yanka*, No. 11, 1979, pp.11-12).

Women's maternal role within the family is frequently linked to female politicisation. As one activist explains, the importance of raising women's political consciousness arises from their responsibility for the education of their children, the 'future builders of the new society':

Raising the political level and consciousness is an important part of zhensovety work. The sailors' wives, as all Soviet people, must deepen their knowledge, learn the historical glory of the Communist Party, the important decisions of the Central Committee and government. It is necessary that Soviet women should know all about events abroad and in our country to raise their consciousness. After all, they have the responsibility to educate their children, the future builders of the new society. That is why the zhensovet pays attention constantly to this part of their activity[9]. (Koval', 1961, p.14)

This suggests that politicisation is not intrinsically important to women as women, rather to women as mothers. This underlines the apparently contradictory role of the zhensovety evident from the socio-political area of their activity. On the one hand the zhensovety aim to politicise women, yet on the other do so much to perpetuate existing gender divisions. Female politicisation is strait-jacketed by the biological role being conflated with social roles. This seems to give little space in zhensovety activity for the emergence of a critical female collective consciousness. This possibility however, will not be entirely dismissed without first considering the zhensovety as a pressure group on behalf of women.

NOTES

1. It should be noted however, that there is a Soviet tradition of 'subbotniks'—groups of volunteers, both male and female, who work on a particular project in their locality.
2. In Chelyabinskaya *oblast'* fifteen zhensovety took part in the 2nd Regional 'Exhibition of Flowers' (Pavolva and Chernyadeva, in Kuznetsova ed., 1961, p.17). During the same period the zhensovet in Barishskii *raion* (Ul'yanovskaya *oblast'*) was also organising flowers. A competition and exhibition of flowers marking the 20th anniversary of Soviet Lithuania, is recorded in the context of witness to 'the growth of the cultural level' (Dobrodzeene, 1961, p.49).
3. Similar claims are made for Batetskii *raion* (Novgorodskaya *oblast'*). 'The zhensovet has had not a little success. It is pleasant to walk along the clean, green streets of the village to find a clean school, with a comfortable library which has a rich fund of books . . . they even say in the village that family squabbles occur less often' (*Krest'yanka*, No. 1, 1980, p.28).
4. A report of a *sovkhoz* zhensovet in Yampol'skii *raion* (Vinnitskaya *oblast'*) claims: 'a drunk who has to account for himself before the zhensovet, does not want to a second time' (*Krest'yanka*, No.10, 1980, p.10).
5. Married women with children have been calculated to spend 8.2 hours per week on self-education and raising their cultural level, compared to the 20.1 hours of married men (E. E. Gruzdeva, *Rabochii Klass i Sovremennyo Mir*, No. 2, 1975, p.96).
6. Increasing concern has been expressed about the lack of male influence, especially on boys. In some areas 'fathers' councils' have been set up to encourage fathers to participate in school activities (Sheinina, 1980, p.28).
7. This is the only reference found to men attending zhensovety meetings apart from male speakers.
    (Stoyankina, 1962, pp.24-5) provides a number of similar examples of help given to individual women. In one case the Chair of a zhensovet, out late one night, was stopped by a woman evidently in some distress. The Chair did her 'social duty' and took the woman home, where over a cup of tea she found out that the jealousy of the woman's husband prevented her from having any social life. The zhensovet was able to resolve the situation.
8. Yakolev, Dr. of Law (Head of Sector USSR Academy of Sciences)

expresses this functionalist view of the family by writing: 'the disorganisation of the family, leads to juvenile crime' (trans. *CDSP,* Vol. XXX, No. 1, 1978, p.14).

The pre-congress discussion for the 26th Congress CPSU included concern with 'effective demographic policies, to promote the strengthening of the family as an important cell of Soviet society' (quoted in 'Vy Nuzhny Drug Druga', Semeinye stranitsy, *Rabotnitsa,* No. 2, 1981, p.24).

9. This is suported by Soviet research. One survey shows that 45.5 per cent of women, compared to 25 per cent of men, spend time talking to their children about political and societal events (Novikova *et al.,* 1978, p.64).

Women are frequently seen as the pivot of the family, both in respect to their children and their husbands. This is illustrated for example, in an article about female farm workers which puts 'caring for women' in the context: 'on this, is dependent the "dreams of the future" and how the husband works' (*Sovetskaya Zhenshchina,* No. 10, 1980, p.3).

7 The Zhensovety: A Pressure Group for Women?

Do the zhensovety have the potential to develop a collective female consciousness? This chapter considers the zhensovety as a pressure group and looks at the consciousness of their activists. This is done in the context of whether zhensovety activities amount to 'women's work' on behalf of the party, or whether the existence of the zhensovety in itself as a 'women-only' body improves the quality of women's lives. If the latter is the case, then it is possible that zhensovety activists put pressure on the party on behalf of women. This in turn would suggest that their role amounts to more than implementation of party policy. This is where the attitude of the activists themselves becomes relevant. Do they have a consciousness of acting with, and on behalf of other women—in other words, a solidarity or sense of 'sisterhood'[1]—that goes beyond their official 'women's work'? If it can be shown that the zhensovety do act as a pressure group, especially within this sense of self-identity as women, there will be support for the proposition that they are potential agents for change in women's consciousness. In this sense the zhensovety could be seen as contributing to women's politicisation. We begin by looking at the zhensovety as a pressure group with respect to two areas of their activity: the workplace and child care.

THE ZHENSOVETY AS A PRESSURE GROUP

In the Workplace
The 'production sectors' of the zhensovety intervene as a

pressure group in the workplace in two ways. One is to raise women's status, the other to ensure that legislation on women's working conditions is implemented. This means that they try to 'improve the facilities and conditions of the woman worker' (Tatarinova, 1968, p.97). It is this aspect of the zhensovety which is picked up by Richard Stites (1978, pp.414-5). 'Their purpose is for bettering the conditions of life . . . by means of inspections, evaluations and recommendations'. The question which must be posed is for what purpose? Is the main concern to improve the quantity and quality of production, as suggested by Blekher? Or is it to make life easier for women?

The zhensovety frequently intervene to improve women's working conditions. In many cases this means ensuring the provision of agreed facilities such as creches. Undoubtedly much of this activity can be construed as taking place in the interests of higher productivity. In one *kolkhoz* for example, the initiative of the zhensovet Chair led to medical treatment being available at the *kolkhoz* on certain days, 'to prevent time being lost in attending the hospital' for minor ailments and treatments (*Krest'yanka*, No. 11, 1978, p.22). Some zhensovety arrange eating facilities at the workplace for similar reasons. At one factory the zhensovet got the management to organise a canteen, 'so that women could save the time spent at home on preparing food' (Stoyankina, 1962, p.21). Similarly, a bakery was provided at another kolkhoz to save the women ten hours baking time (*Krest'yanka*, No. 1, 1978, pp.23-4). Whilst such intervention has the effect of improving women's productivity (the time saved in baking will be spent at the *kolkhoz*) not all intervention falls into this category. It can also improve the quality of women's lives. It is in this context that zhensovety activists refer to carrying on the caring traditions of the *zhenotdel*.

As in the first years of Soviet power, the zhensovety watch over the interests of both peasants and workers . . . the form of their care has changed. It no longer concerns illiteracy, but now the zhensovety of the 1970s have become true helpers of the trades unions. They engage in protecting women's work by following the occupational status of women, and organising leisure for them and their children'. (*Otchizna*, March 1981, p.4)

Some maintain that this is now the main concern of their work (*Krest'yanka*, No. 1, 1978). One form this takes is improving rest and leisure facilities for women workers. The Rhizhskovo zhensovet at the Lenin works (Pamir) for example, organised extra rest periods for women, and together with 'health specialists' sought to reduce women's working fatigue (Rusakova *et al.*, 1979, p.6). In Belgorod *oblast'*, the *raion* zhensovet discovered women *kolkhozniks* were not taking advantage of the leisure arrangements. The tourist outings were inconvenient: either the women were busy with housework, or lacked confidence to go on their own. Zhensovet activists suggested that women could go in groups with their friends, or with members of their families[2]. In another case, a zhensovet member in Bobrinka village (Omsk district), suggested the creation of a 'rest zone' outside the village, consisting of a playing area for children, a garden and seats, where women could go on a Sunday to read and meet other women. The zhensovet put the proposal to the *kolkhoz* management and to the local party committee. The latter recommended the scheme: 'the women thought it up, I think all communists support their suggestion' (*Krest'yanka*, No. 11, 1980).

Despite the tone of benevolent paternalism in this response, the example serves to illustrate that the zhensovety do act on behalf of women workers. In some cases, this has brought zhensovety activists into conflict with management. To support women they have had to oppose the practice of (male) managers and trade union officials. In one sanatorium, 'The Donbass' (Slavgaskurot) with a work force 90 per cent female, the zhensovet had unsuccessfully criticised the management for ignoring women's 'special needs' and had to take their complaints to the local party committee before their demands were met (*Krest'yanka*, No. 11, 1978). In other cases the zhensovety have come into conflict with the trades unions. At a *sovkhoz* (collective farm) in Moldavia for example, vineyard workers were expected to carry loads above the legally permitted weight. Eventually the *sovkhoz* management upheld the law, but not until the zhensovet Chair had challenged the trade union representative in a 'heated discussion', with 'You don't have the right to ignore Soviet law . . . . But we will stand up for our rights' (*Otchizna*, 1981, p.5). Such examples serve to illustrate that the zhensovety do have the potential to act as a form of pressure group on behalf of women.

Child Care

The previous chapter showed how the zhensovety support mothers to enable them to raise their productivity. For some there is no ambiguity about this. One report of a 'round table' discussion of zhensovety activists states that 'The zhensovety try to ensure that women's children are well looked after so that the women can work well' (*Krest'yanka,* No. 8, 1976, p.10). In Lithuania a report claims that the zhensovety should demand kindergartens, especially at harvest time (Dobrodzeene, 1961, p.50). But to what extent does this investigation also benefit mothers? Pre-school provision in particular is acknowledged to be severely inadequate both in quality and quantity[3]. Zhensovety activists frequently confront barriers to adequate child care provision, and it is this, and their own attitudes, which prevent their activity being reduced to support for higher productivity. In a number of sources zhensovety activists raise sharply the difficulties women face to get adequate child care. Some activists make their dissatisfaction public with complaints to the press and the women's journals. In one letter to *Krest'yanka* for example, the Chair of the zhensovet in Pokroskoe village (Firov *raion*), gives details of her zhensovet activity over a period of fifteen years. She complains that given the number of young, energetic women in the village, the zhensovety would have been more effective if there had been child-care facilities. She writes that, with no nursery or kindergarten, 'mothers of children up to six years are practically tied to the home'. She points out that this not only prevents them from being less productive, it also stops them for taking part in social activities at the Palace of Culture. She reports that after appealing to the *raikom* and the *oblast'* party, the zhensovet thought it had made progress. 'The Firov *raikom* held a meeting at our village soviet. We invited young mothers. It was quite pleasant for the management to have to hear what they had to say . . . it was agreed that a nursery was needed, and a decision was taken to build one'. The sting comes in the tail of the letter. 'But, we celebrated too early. The appropriate sector of the village soviet did not confirm the decision. Now the nursery will not be built until 1980, [four years later] and even that is open to question' (*Krest'yanka*, No. 9, 1976, p.24).

Whilst this example shows the limitations of zhensovety authority as a pressure group, other sources claim more success[4]. Pressure on local party and soviet committees has produced results. The correspondent interviewed at *Rabotnitsa* instanced the Perine nursery built as a result of local zhensovet complaints to their party organisation. In Moldavia the claimed growth of five times over a period of seven years still meant that the number of kindergartens and nurseries was inadequate. The republic zhensovet got the Moldavian Ministry of Construction to introduce a competition for the best building as a means of encouraging better provision[5]. A similar idea was introduced in the new town of Ukhta. Despite the average age of the town being twenty-eight, pre-school places were inadequate. The zhensovet 'took control' of the building programme forcing over-fulfilment of the plan (Rusakova *et al.*, 1979, p.6). Thus the zhensovety can influence the allocation of resources. As women are expected to work, whatever the child-care arrangements, improvements by zhensovety activity must benefit them directly. Tallya's (1975, p.236) assessment is that the zhensovety have improved social service provision for women 'significantly'.

The zhensovety then are prepared to support women even when this brings them into conflict with others. In this respect their intervention tends to support Richard Stites' description of the zhensovety, and indicates the limitations of Feiga Blekher's assessment which denies this supportive role. But the proviso must be made that any zhensovety role as a pressure group is limited. Activities remain within the bounds of legitimate concerns agreed elsewhere, not by the zhensovety or by women themselves. But this does not necessarily mean that the consciousness of individual activists is similarly constrained.

ZHENSOVETY ACTIVISTS AND CONSCIOUSNESS

Consciousness by activists is generally construed in the Soviet sense of commitment to socialism. It is this interpretation which is evident in a letter from two village women to *Krest'yanka* (No. 7, 1976, p.24). Their club, set up by the village zhensovet, 'not only changed our village and the character of village work, but also the consciousness of the women workers . . . after all it is all inter-connected'. As we know, similar claims have been made about the zhensovety since the early days (Kuriedov, 1959; Sibrayeva, 1961).

This, though, is not the only understanding of consciousness. In Lithuania a zhensovet activist makes the point that it is important for zhensovety committee members to raise relevant issues themselves with, for example, the management of their *kolkhoz*, rather than have the local party do so on their behalf. Her assertion that women should become used to such discussions indicates an awareness of the value of confidence building and developing skills for political participation. Indeed, the suggestion is made in the context of chastising party leaders, who 'without any basis, are afraid to promote women to leading work' (Dobrodzeene, 1961, p.50). Similarly, a party worker points out that women making their own complaints to the bureaucracy will contribute to their political awareness (Zel'dich in Kuznetsova ed., 1961, pp.31-2).

Gender awareness, and a sense of 'sisterhood'—a solidarity with other women—is also found in the writings of some activists. In one factory zhensovet, female workers objected to their being responsible for orderliness at work. They pointed out that male workers contributed to the disorder, and would benefit from any clearing up. Their protest led to the men taking part (Kuznetsova ed., 1961. p.23).

Soviet women also refer to one another as 'sisters', especially during the early period of the zhensovety. The first Uzbek Women's Congress (1958) was addressed by a former member of the zhenotdel as 'Beloved sisters'. Other delegates used 'Our sisters'.[6] Activists have referred to the benefits of all-women get-togethers (Belyaeva, 1962, p.20). Others are quite explicit that their main priority is their support to other women. Gurtovnik (1963, p.479), one of the early activists, in reporting on her work in the Urals, emphasises her personal commitment: 'I will carry out work amongst women, whilst I have enough strength'. The Chair of the trades union commission in Moscow said she was motivated to help the women at her place of work, and claimed 'I always stand up for women'. However, she thought that her comment that women were the best workers was probably subjective. The staff member of *Rabotnitsa* was keen to emphasise her point that 'It is women who are helping the mass of women'. Members of a zhensovet recently formed on a *kolkhoz* in the autonomous republic of Checheno Ingushskaya, 'after a long argument' agreed their main responsibility was to 'stir up all women, even the most reticent, and to establish women's rights in the home and at work' (*Krest'yanka*, No. 9, 1980, p.27). Thus some zhensovety at least carry on the tradition of the early groups which, in the words of one of them, resolved that 'they would open men's eyes . . . to show them, that everyone, including women, can be agitators' (Kuznetsova, 1962, p.9). The first year's report of this particular zhensovet concluded that their main achievement had been to 'help women believe in their own strength', and that 'the women's relationships became warmer amongst themselves'. This is supported by Stoyankina's (1962, p.14) overall view of the early zhensovety, in which she claims that their growth helped 'educate women in a sense of "collectivism, friendship and mutual support" '.

Although such attitudes, at least in written sources, are few, they do exist. Whilst it is evident that the zhensovety have contributed little nationally to gender awareness, nor has that been the intention, it is all the more significant that individuals have this consciousness. This awareness amongst some activists which governs their work in the zhensovety, suggests that the view which considers that Soviet women lack the means for 'female bonding' can be modified. At the same time, this gender identity is not sufficiently developed to counteract the effects of the political culture in which activity is geared for implementation of party policy, and the prevalence of zhensovety activity fosters existing gender roles.

NOTES

1. Numerous organisations exist elsewhere without men, as for example the Women's Institute in Britain, which whilst campaigning on issues of importance to women, do not necessarily engender a political consciousness. As Anne Oakley (1981, p.278) has written, 'Female solidarity does not automatically mean a feminist consciousness. Women who co-operate with one another are not necessarily aware that the covert bond indexes a common oppression'. On the other hand, without a sense of solidarity, a feminist consciousness is unlikely to develop.
2. The report concludes: 'Now women willingly go on holiday . . . especially to the Baltic' (Litochenko, Chair 'Frunze' Kolkhoz zhensovet, 'Round Table Discussion', *Krest'yanka*, No. 8, 1976, p.11).
3. See for example references to: Uzbekistan, Nasriddinova (1964), p.170; Turkmenia, Myatieva (1973), p.13; Rostovskaya oblast' (Moldavia), *Krest'yanka*, No. 2 (1975), p.2: Novogorodskaya oblast', *Krest'yanka*, No. 1 (1980), p.28.
4. The zhensovty have been claiming such success since their earliest days. P. B. Prokop'eva, Chair of a zhensovet, reported to the 1st Buryat Women's Congress that five nurseries had opened due to the zhensovet (*Iii Buryatskoi S'ezd Zhenshchin*, 1961, p.90).
5. The report refers to the lack of funds for pre-school facilities and claims that in the small villages builders receive higher premiums for industrial building than for children's institutions.
6. At the 1st Buryat Women's Congress held in 1960, the delegates addressed one another as 'Dear Friends' (*podrugy*), and the republic zhensovet sent greetings to 'Comrades, friends and sisters' (*Iii S'ezd Buryatskoi Zhenshchin*, 1961, p.7). At later congresses less use of such forms is made, with 'comrade' being used instead.

Conclusion

We have established that 'women-only' groups exist in the USSR involving large numbers of Soviet women. They pursue a policy of raising women's political consciousness in the context of a policy of equal opportunity. Yet this extensive informal activity fails to affect positively the low numbers of women in positions of political leadership. The reason for this was sought from two perspectives. The first was to estimate the effectiveness of the zhensovety in terms of their official aim of raising women's consciousness as 'Active builders of Communism'—a contribution to the 'New Communist Woman'. The second was to evaluate zhensovety potential for developing a gender awareness of the generality of women's position.

THE NEW COMMUNIST WOMAN

The 'New Communist Woman' is a product of women entering the economic world, being politically conscious and socially active, whilst retaining those feminine qualities associated particularly with motherhood. The activities of the zhensovety are geared for this purpose. Mobilisation and enlightenment are the twin prongs for its execution. We considered, though, whether more emphasis was placed on mobilising women for the interests of production, than on their political and social development. The economic activity of the zhensovety encouraged women to enter paid work and to increase their productivity. At the same time it helped women raise their qualifications. Individual zhensovety claim successes. The mushrooming of the zhensovety in the Khrushchev period coincided with a significant increase of women in the work force. However, calls to increase productivity continue unabated, and unmechanised labour is still performed predominantly by women. Women are confronted daily with the problem of juggling parental responsibilities with those of their paid work. Despite thirty years existence of the zhensovety, inadequate child-care facilities continue. In some regions the problem is so dire that women have opted for work at home. The party has now adopted a policy of a shorter working day for women, and part-time work. These realities put zhensovety claims into perspective.

Economic concerns are a major activity of the zhensovety, and to that extent warrant the claim made by Feiga Blekher (1979, p.22), that mobilisation is their main role. This assessment, however, ignores those activities which benefit women, and the efforts by activists to defend women's interests in the workplace. Mobilisation is not the sole function of the zhensovety, either in theory or in practice. Reducing the role of the zhensovety to meeting the pragmatic needs of the economy denies the ideological framework within which the zhensovety exist. Their efforts to encourage women to participate more in the economy cannot be divorced entirely from the theory that this is a crucial factor in raising female consciousness.

There is also the other strand to mobilisation—political activity. It is quite clear that much of this activity is geared to mobilising women for implementation of the current economic plan. But again this is not the whole story. Political consciousness is judged also by knowledge and support of the theory and policy of the CPSU, the apex being party membership. How successful have the zhensovety been in terms of Soviet politicisation? It could be expected that the extensive political enlightenment would make women suitable candidates for the CPSU. Yet, despite a few claims to the contrary, there is little direct evidence of the zhensovety contributing to party membership. No data are available to ascertain whether the social work experience provided by the zhensovety has been a factor in the steady increase in female membership during this period.

Awareness that female politicisation would be fostered by actual participation is highlighted by its rarity and by the generally passive nature of political enlightenment. Activity in the Peace Fund in recent years does not give women either a new political image or the skills required for a political career. Nor do the posts of responsibility in the zhensovety. Though the flexibility of zhensovety structure does enable other women to gain confidence and skills, in the main, where identifiable, it is those who already have experience who fill these posts. The zhensovety as such are a vehicle for female members of the party and soviets to fulfil their social responsibilities.

Advance of women's politicisation is further restrained by the social activity of the zhensovety. Social activities comprise two groups: those aiming to raise the level of culture as a contribution to political consciousness; and those which foster traditional gender skills. It is probable that many women have benefitted from the cultural activities which attempt to broaden women's horizons. They take a poor second place though to the other social activities. Home management and child care in particular receive much attention by the zhensovety, In addition, zhensovety have responsibility for order in the social and physical environment. It could be argued that this responsibility in the public sphere represents a strategic step in women's political advance. But the context of zhensovety reports suggests instead that it is an extension of female gender roles in the private sphere and as such does little to mark an image of women as capable of holding posts in the political leadership. Thus the efficacy of the zhensovety in consciousness raising is undermined by a major part of their own work.

ZHENSOVETY POTENTIAL FOR A FEMALE SELF-IDENTITY

Zhensovety characterisation as 'ad hoc', 'spontaneous', 'independent', 'women-only' groups whose members work 'on their own initiative', was examined in the context of women's autonomy. Although there is no central directive for the zhensovety, these features were found to fall far short of criteria common to Western feminist groups. Zhensovety organisation and structure is generally hierarchial, with the position of Chair echoing the status of party bodies. The 'spontaneous', 'ad hoc' nature of the zhensovety was not so much by design as accident. The policy of 'differentiation' from which they arose was fostered by the party leadership. The diversity of the zhensovety is partly accounted for by the low status awarded 'women's work' by the party organisations, which in some regions meant that formation of a zhensovet was left to women themselves. 'Initiative' is both applauded and devalued. Calls for formalisation and greater party involvement now seem likely to be realised following Gorbachev's remarks at the 27th Congress.

The characteristic of 'independence' was posed in terms of zhensovety relationship to the CPSU. The experience of the Western women's movement regarding autonomous space can be seen as particularly pertinent in Soviet society with the pervasive political culture of the CPSU, and its male hegemony. The absence of a formal structural relationship gives the zhensovety some diversity. But party input is ensured through its self-appointed vanguard role in Soviet society, and by party members within the zhensovety whose role is to implement party policy. Not only do the zhensovety seek to implement party policy, party norms are their guidelines. In this sense the zhensovety are not 'independent' and apparently bear out Jancar's (1978, p.110) assertion that Soviet women do not have the space 'to discover female bonding' to 'mobilise politically'.

However, whilst the zhensovety are part of the political network, they have the means to make inputs on behalf of women whom they represent legitimately. The zhensovety benefit individual women, particularly the single parent and heroine mother. The task of supporting women as well as the party can present zhensovety activists with a latent conflict of interests. Sometimes, as we have seen, this has entailed actual conflict. This in itself does not constitute autonomy—in supporting women's rights, activists are implementing official party policy. It does suggest, though, that activists as individual women are not simply the mouthpieces of their (male) superiors. In this sense they exert a semblance of 'independence' and act on their own 'initiative'. Added to this is the solidarity with other women, the sense of sisterhood expressed by some activists. There are also references to women critically conscious of their position *vis à vis* men, perceiving this as an important role for the zhensovety. Although such attitudes are expressed infrequently, at least in the written materials available, their existence, together with the women-only nature of the zhensovety, means that, in theory at least, they have the potential collectively to develop a female consciousness.

The restraints on this potential can be illustrated by the example of child care. Within the continuing sexual division of labour, inadequate child care is of vital concern to women. Whilst this activity might well have the potential for awareness that women's interests are poorly served, it is restrained by the accepted parameters of party norms about women. Where zhensovety activists take officials to task they act on behalf of women, but within the confines of accepted party guidelines. Intervention by the zhensovety usually means ensuring that the plans are implemented, not that resources are re-allocated. Their support of individual women entails the zhensovety carrying out the welfare responsibilities of state bodies on a voluntary basis. This means that women are being used to support other women in the community in a way traditionally accepted as 'women's work'. The zhensovety institutionalise this notion.

Whilst real restraints are imposed by the political culture in which they operate, especially in respect to mobilisation and reinforcement of traditional roles, the support given by women to women cannot be reduced to party mobilisation. This yields a more complex picture of the zhensovety than that presented in current Western sources. The zhensovety are not reducible to a mobilising agent (Blekher, 1979, p.22), nor is their whole concern to represent women's issues in the political sphere rather than the economy (Lapidus, 1978, p.208). They combine both. In conjunction with their social activities this gives the zhensovety a wide-ranging role. Furthermore, 'female bonding' is not an impossibility.

THE ZHENSOVETY AND CONTRADICTIONS IN SOVIET POLICY

The zhensovety are inherently contradictory. They aim to ease women's lives—with some success—yet mobilisation contributes to the pressures and burdens of their daily lives. It is impractical to expect women to embrace additional responsibilities without radical transformation in the sexual division of labour. This the zhensovety do not seriously confront. The zhensovety aim to politicise women and develop the necessary skills for political activity, advance women's consciousness and status in society, and yet they reinforce those gender roles which preclude women from that activity. The social activity of the activists is understood to be an expression of their politicisation, but the content of that activity ghettoises it as women's work. They have a semblance of 'independence', but in essence are controlled by the political culture of the CPSU. These contradictions prevent the zhensovety from acting as a bridge between the formal and informal political structures. The contradictions also prevent the zhensovety from being an effective agent in raising female consciousness. By reinforcing gender roles the zhensovety reinforce women's subordination. In this respect the zhensovety are themselves agents of sexism in Soviet society.

The contradictions reflect conflicting Soviet policy on women, which in turn arises from a theory which supports sexual equality, but retains a belief in biologism. Whilst child-rearing remains the 'natural' province of women, Soviet institutions, and that includes the zhensovety, will direct their attention to easing women's role rather than changing it. Biologism not only provides the justification for women's limited participation, it also prevents the re-structuring of the sexual division within the family. Biologism is legitimised by 'motherhood' not parenthood, being identified in the Soviet constitution. The zhensovety indicate the transient and limited concept of women as a specific category. They pay no attention to the effect on equality of sexual relations. Whilst Soviet theory continues to deny the relationship of personal and sexual politics to social attitudes; whilst women are denied the space to conceptualise their experiences; the sexism which prevents women being politically equal to men will continue.

THE ZHENSOVETY: WHAT THEY TELL US ABOUT WOMEN IN POLITICS

What then has research into the women's 'social' organisations contributed to our knowledge of women's place in the Soviet political structure?[1] The USSR has done much to show that women can be as politically active as men, by broadening the concept of what constitutes politics and by encouraging women to participate. A range of women's issues previously confined to the private sphere now exists in the public. We have seen that despite all the pressure on women's time, they are prepared to participate in community politics. The extensive activity of women in the community means there is no shortage of women with the specified experience required for party membership. This experience is no doubt reflected in the steady increase of women in the party. But the proportion of women to men reached so far in no way reflects the proportion of women participating in social organisations. Women's issues have been retained as the province of women. And women have not gained access to those power positions which define and prioritise these issues. The low status of the zhensovety illustrates the inferior status of 'low' politics. Defining women as politically active by instancing their participation in production and social organisations obfuscates their absence from the policy-making political leadership.

The traditional division between private and public has been transferred, virtually intact, to a division between 'high' and 'low' public politics. 'Women's issues' meet this barrier, just as women themselves do. Thus the male/female dichotomy within politics continues, it is only the demarcation lines which have shifted. The Soviet experience serves to indicate to women elsewhere that broadening political parameters and bringing women into public activity, even in equal numbers to men, can be contained within the existing traditional model of power, a power which is male and which continues to limit and omit women. It is not sufficient for women to be in politics. They have to be in the politics of power, both to participate as women and to change the very nature of that power which serves to preclude women. Individual women in positions of power are unlikely to challenge the male hegemony without a support network of women who are gender-conscious, autonomous from men. For the zhensovety to become such a body, requires women within the CPSU to make the case.

The discriminatory practices and ideology of the CPSU counteract attempts to politicise women. Women are not encouraged to seek high office. The unwillingness to implement party policy on sexual equality suggests a practice that is sexist. Within the context of the vanguard role, sexist practice by the party means it is contributing to the perpetuation of the commonsense ideology and practice of sexism in Soviet society. To fulfil its vanguard role, the CPSU must be seen to break with its own discrimination. It is crucial that women be seen in positions of political power. Initially it is only the *nomenklatura* which can ensure they are. Ignoring the question perpetuates the sexism.

The zhensovety show that no official female dimension yet exists to challenge the present concept of equality. Without alternative theory there is unlikely to be a fundamental change in the position of women in political power. Soviet socialism does not appear in essence to have lessened the hold of patriarchy. Currently there is little to suggest that the male leadership of the CPSU intends to surrender its political monopoly, either as an elite or as males. It is predominantly men who decide whether women-only groups are desirable and, if they are, on what terms. It is men who determine the nature of the relationship between the groups and other bodies. The idea of an organisation existing as autonomous from the CPSU has become enshrined as an anachronism. Autonomy would require change in the party's theory of leadership. Autonomy for women, as for any other social grouping, would undermine the party's interpretation of its vanguard role. Unless confronted by a stronger lobby within the legitimate political culture, the male leadership is unlikely to relinquish power by encouraging women to participate. It is improbable that the zhensovety can present such a challenge. But we in the West should not presume a monopoly of wisdom. Change in the Soviet system is not only dependent on influence from outside. The zhensovety have already brought about some changes in women's lives. In this they support Friedgut's (1979, p.242) premiss that social organisations may be of some influence.

The latent conflict of the inconsistencies in Soviet policy could enhance zhensovety contribution to change[2]. There is little sign of the emergence of a collective sense of gender identity capable of challenging the existing parameters of the female image. Yet the contradictions in that image, manifest in the contradictions of the zhensovety, may themselves demand resolution. The 'woman question' continues to present the party with a dilemma. Party commitment to equality is equated with the legitimacy of the system. Post-revolutionary trauma, war, industrial priorities, have all enabled the resolution of full equality to be suspended. The concept of mature socialism has extended the day of reckoning. But this now takes place in a context of increasing visibility of women. The very advances that women have made in the political, educational and other institutions in Soviet society confirm the policy of sexual equality and at the same time highlight its failures. As women become more visible, so do their demands for a better quality of life. The desire to take life easier, however, let alone participate in the hitherto male domains of high politics, conflict with the current demands made on women to raise the birth rate, and increase production, in addition to expanding their socio-political activity. Not only is it recognised that women are unable to combine all these roles[3] women themselves refuse to. They restrict the number of children and do not challenge their under-representation in political posts. The introduction of part-time work for women potentially undermines the basis of Soviet theory which marks participation in production as the vital factor of sexual equality. Given the need to retain an ideology of sexual equality as a legitimating factor for socialist society, it is questionable how far present policies can be pursued. Hence the dilemma which remains endemic whilst Soviet theory retains the contradiction of a sexual equality based on biologism. To resolve this, women require both the autonomy to mobilise politically and to accede to positions of political power to challenge the sexism of Soviet society.

NOTES

1. A number of associated questions not included in this study would benefit this discussion, namely: the relationship between women's participation, democracy and the nature of the Soviet system; the role of women's participation in civil society as a focus of change in political systems; and an examination of the Soviet critique of 'bourgeois feminism'.
2. Sacks (1976) suggests that there is a growing conflict between an image of 'idealized femininity' and women's industrial role, which could lead to women's awareness and organisation.
3. Yuri Riurikov (1977b) for example, suggests that it is the incompatibility of these roles which explains the low birth rate.

Appendices

APPENDIX 1.i

Table 6: Female Candidate Members of the Central Committee CPSU 1986

Name	Date of Birth	Date CAC	Elected candidate	Post
BOROVIKOVA Z. I.			1986	1st Sec. Kurganinsk *raikom*, Krasnodar, Krai, RSFSR
BRYZGA Lidiya Dmitrievna	1943	1981	1986	Milking machine operator, *kolkhoz, Brest raion*, Brest *oblast'*, Belorussia
GELLERT Natal'ya Valdimirovna	1953		1986	Tractor driver, *sovkhoz*, Kurgal'dzinskii *raion*, Tselinograd *oblast'*, Kazakhstan
IVANOVA Tat'yana Georgievna	1940		1981	Deputy Chair, Presidium, RSFSR Council of Ministers; 1st secretary, Kalinin *raikom*, Moscow
KASIMOVA Valentina Aleksandrovna	1944	1981	1986	Assembler, Tula Plant for Electrical Components, RSFSR
KIRGIZBAEVA Tukhtakhon Bazarovna	1942		1986	Leader cotton team, *sovkhoz*, Syrdar'ya *raion*, Syrdar'ya *obl.*, Uzbekistan
KLEIKO S. V.				
MERKULOVA Galina V.			1986	Brigade leader of painters, Vladivostock House Building Combine, Primor'ie Krai, RSFSR
PARSHINA Valentina Romanovna	1937		1981	Brigade leader, vegetable growing, *sovkhoz*, Tesno *raion*, Leningrad *oblast'*

Sources: *Pravda* (7 March, 1986); Sergei Belitsky; Valerii Konovalov; Herwig Kraus. 'CPSU CC candidate members elected by the 27th Party Congress in March 1986', *Radio Liberty*, No. 16, RL 151/86 (16 April 1986).

APPENDIX 1.ii

Table 7: *Women Elected to the Central Auditing Commission, 1986*

Name	Date of Birth	Date Elected	Post
AVAKYAN Gayane Avetikovna	1954	1986	Railway operator, Yerevan, Armenia
BALYKOVA Lyutsiya Kuz'mnichna		1986	Teacher, Bol'shie Uki *raion*, Omsk *oblast'*, RSFSR
BEISHEKEEVA Zaina Satybaldievna		1986	Senior stockman, *sovkhoz*, Dzhety-Oguz *raion*, Issyk-Kul' *oblast'*, Kirghizia
GULOVA Zulaikho Sokhibnazarovna		1986	Brigade leader, *kolkhoz*, Ordzhonikizeabad *raion*, Tadjhikistan
KAS'YANOVA G. V.		1986	
KOMAROVA Domna Pavlovna	1920	1966	Minister of Social Security, RSFSR
KRASNENKOVA V. F.		1986	
MAKSIMKINA Ada Mikhailovna		1986	Radio equipment adjuster, Riga, Latvia
NIZOVTSEVA Alla Afanas'evna		1986	Secretary, Moscow *gorkom;* Deputy Chair, Central Auditing Commissn.
ODOBESKU Vera Segeevna	1934	1986	Cutter, Kishniev Footwear Production Association, Moldavia
RYNDINA Antonina Nikolaevna	1942	1981	Brigade leader, Shilovo *raion*, Ryazan *oblast'*, RSFSR
RZAEVA Tamilla Nariman Kyzy		1986	Petrol/gas extraction operator, Kirov *raion*, Baku, Azerbaidjan
SHCHERBAKOVA Nina Nikolaevna		1986	Weaver, cotton combine, Moscow
SHVETSOVA Lyudmilla Ivanovna		1986	Secretary, Central Committee Komsomol; Chair, Central Council, All Union Pioneer Organisatn *imeni* 'V. I. Lenin'
SMIRNOVA Lyubov' Evgen'evna		1986	Operator, Kazan' Productn Assn. Tatar ASSR, RSFSR

APPENDIX 1.ii Table 7 contd.

Name	Date of Birth	Date Elected	Post
SNETKOVA T. I.		1986	Leningrad *obkom*
STRUL'PINENE Zinaida A.		1986	Weaver, Linas Production Association, Panevezhis, Lithuania
SUKHORUCHENKOVA Galina Fedorovna		1986	Secretary, All Union Central Council of Trades Unions
TROFIMOVA Tat'yana Gavrilovna		1986	Operator, petrol refinery, Bashkir ASSR, RSFSR

Sources: based on data in: *Pravda* (4 March 1981; 7 March 1986); Sergei Belitsky; Valerii Konovalov; Herwig Kraus, *Radio Liberty*, No. 16., RL 156/86 (14 April 1986).

APPENDIX 2: CORRESPONDENCE FROM SOVIET WOMEN'S COMMITTEE

Genia Browning,
Great Britain

Dear Genia,

I am awfully sorry I could not answer your letter earlier. Frankly, I was very busy first with a business trip and then with my work in the Soviet Women's Committee.

I tried hard to find some printed materials about the women's councils in English, which you are interested in, but unfortunately could not do so. So, I decided to describe the activities of the women's councils in our country and I hope this information will be enough for you and your research in the University.

The women's councils are independent public organisations on a voluntary basis. They are set up at industrial plants, collective and state farms, offices, military units, house management offices and house management committees.

The women's councils are elected by a general asembly of women, who vote by a show of hands, for a term of one or two years. The number of councillors varies from five to thirty and depends on the range of activities. The women's councils regularly (usually once a year) give an account of their activities before their electorate.

The women's councils are set up at the level of a town, a district, a region and a republic. Such councils are functioning at many Ukrainian regions, at numerous regions and autonomous republics of the Russian Federation, Byelorussia, Moldavia and the republics in Soviet Central Asia. They are also elected by the show of hands at women's conferences, meetings and congresses at the level of a town, a district, a region or a republic.

Together with trade unions women's councils work to improve the working conditions for women and follow their production achievements. They contribute to the construction of the child-care centres by organising checkups and the day of voluntary work without payment at the construction sites and help improve the everyday services for women.

They attach great significance to the raising of a young generation. The councils organise lectures for mothers at the child-care centres, courses of lectures on educational methods for parents at the clubs and the House of Culture and give all possible assistance to the PTA committees. Jointly with the house and street management committees they organise playing grounds, clubs and playing rooms at the housing administration committeees for children at the places of their residence. This work of theirs is not paid for, they do it of their own volition.

Over the past few years the women's councils have been increasingly founding women's clubs which are engaged in broad propaganda and educational activities. In the Chelyabinsk region alone there are 40 such clubs.

And last, but not least, women often turn to the women's councils with their complaints, which always help them in every possible way.

The women's councils' structure is sectoral to ensure their smooth functioning in each field of their activities. The number of sectors depends on the needs and the conditions of work of a collective body which sets up this or that council. Usually, a women's council consists of the production, everyday, cultural and child-care sectors, headed by the members of the women's council.

The women's councils carry out their activities in keeping with a programme, or plan of work, approved of at one of the meetings. In this they are assisted by the women-workers in the production shops and the departments of a factory. (At the big factories, there is a women's council at every production shop, and their chairmen are usually elected to the women's council of a factory).

The production sector checks up the observance of the safety measures of work for women and labour legislation, particularly with regard to would-be mothers and baby-feeding mothers. This sector is concerned with women's promotions, skills and overall supply. At the Ural railway car-building plant in Nizhny Tagil, for example, the women's commission insisted on a five-year programme of activities aimed at easing the working conditions and at improving the living conditions for women. The councils make a tangible contribution to the trade unions' work among women aimed at staging the All-Union Review of the conditions of work, life and leisure for women.

The every-day life sector is concerned with the engineering organisation of the territory of factories and production shops and the afforestation of streets and courts at the factory settlements. The women check up the functioning of public catering enterprises, order and delivery departments and the sales of the ready-to-cook goods, etc. The workers of the sector take care of a factory's hostels. They organise drives for the model flat, model house, model street.

The cultural sector is charged with the functioning of a club, a Palace of Culture, an agitprop room and a library. The members of the sector help organise lectures, meetings, consultations for women, knitting sections, dress-making schools, courses on cooking, parties for women and so on.

Task No. 1 for the child-care sector is to assist schools' administration in organising extra class activities for school children (this sector works in cooperation with the trade union's commission of assistance to a family and a school), to supervise the construction of child-care centres and to work with difficult children.

Women elect their best warm-hearted representatives full of vigour to the women's councils. For many of them the councils became the schools of organisational activities.

The activities of the women's councils are discussed at the annual conferences of women.

Dear Genia. This, I believe, is all what was there to say in brief about the main functions of these organisations. I will be happy to learn that this information is of any value to you.
Sincerely yours
Marina Moskvina

APPENDIX 3.i: THE WORK OF OBLAST' AND LOCAL ZHENSOVETY

i. Plan of Work for Orlovskaya Oblast' Zhensovet: December 1961-August 1962

1. Hold a meeting of the women activists in the oblast on the question 'The participation of women in the propaganda and the realisation of the decisions of the 22nd Congress of the CPSU'.

2. Work out and discuss at the conference of the raion zhensovety the measures for women's participation in the propaganda and realisation of the decisions of the 22nd Congress of the CPSU.

3. At enterprises, building sites, in the kolkhozes and sovkhozes in the house management offices, hold meetings of women about the work of the 22nd Congress of the CPSU and the tasks of women in propaganda and realisation of its decisions (December-January).

4. By studies, disseminate and introduce advanced know-how to ensure the active participation of women in the work of seminars, to be held at the best enterprises, building sites and at the most advanced kolkhozes and sovkhozes, and brigades on farms:

(a) in the brigade of the turner factory for the production of spare parts for agricultural machines which is led by A. K. Uchkova (December).

(b) at the farm sovkhoz 'Pankovskii', Novodereven'skii raion, where the outstanding pig tender of the area, A. F. Komissarova, works.

(c) at the poultry farm of the sovkhoz 'Tyankovskii', Maloarkhangelskii raion, where the leading poultry maid, M. A. Rodina, works.

(d) at the oblast' experimental station (January).

(e) in the brigade of Communist work at building site No. 2. (June).

(f) at the knitted goods factory where the knitter A. V. Vorob'eva works (February-March).

(g) in the kolkhoz 'Red Banner' where the outstanding corn producer in the oblast', P. E. Sapunov, works (February-March).

(h) in the kolkhoz 'Lenin Banner', Dimitrovskii raion (April).

5. Oblast' and raion zhensovety to take part in checking on the winter cattle at the farms of the Kromskii, Mtsenskii, Orlovskii, Bolhovskii and Droskovskii raions (January).

6. Give help to the Orlovskii, Livenskii and Mtsenskii zhensovety with their educational work amongst the women's brigades of the industrial enterprises, building sites and transport; 'We struggle in the name of collective communist work' (December-February).

7. Hold oblast' meetings of sovkhoz and kolkhoz women—participants in the competition for the name of 'collective' and 'shock workers of Communist work'—on the question of 'The participation of village women in fulfilling the commitments taken in 1962' (February).

8. To help the organisations of people's education and the committees of the Komsomol to organise a check in every raion and town on the implementation of universal compulsory education for children (January).

9. Organise children's rooms attached to the house management committees and instal public-spirited women on duty.

10. To check on, and improve with the help of strong zhensovety and their activists, the work of kitchens and semi-prepared food shops (December-March).

11. Organise an inspection to check on the work of

children's institutions and give help to the soviet and management to increase the number of pre-school institutions (December-June).

12. Take part in the seminars for raising the qualifications of workers of pre-school institutions and the preparation of the necessary number of cadres for working in children's kindergarten and nurseries in the kolkhozes and sovkhozes during the time of agricultural work.

13. Listen to accounts of the work of the Droskovskii; Russko-Brodskii and Nikolskii raion zhensovety (January-March).

14. An active part to be taken by the zhensovety in the enterprises and sovkhozes and kolkhozes in the work of the cultural enlightenment organisations in accordance with the decision on propaganda taken at the 22nd Congress CPSU (The whole period).

' "These measures", said M. I. Koval'chuk, chair of the Orlovskaya oblast' zhensovet, "are to be fulfilled successfully" '.

quoted by A. S. Stoyankina, *Zhenskie Sovety* (Moscow, Sovetskaya Rossiya, 1962) pp.9-11.

APPENDIX 3.ii: TASKS FOR LOCAL ZHENSOVETY

Outline reminders sent to the local zhensovety by the Barishskii raion zhensovet to 'help the zhensovety form a "Plan of Work" '.

" 'Raise the level of activity in the struggle for the fulfilment of agreed commitments and the annual plan.

Publicise the best women workers in print, on the radio and at meetings.

Meetings of the zhensovety to discuss those who work poorly, or only half-heartedly.

Aim to speed up the building of kindergartens and nurseries in the villages and towns; carry out on the spot inspections of children's institutions and be directly involved in their supervision.

Check on medical institutions, canteens and shops.

Organise talks for parents on the upbringing of well-behaved children.

Hold evenings for young people and arrange afternoon talks for children.

Arrange 'dejourniers' [duty officers] in the schools and clubs and sport areas.

Invite to zhensovety meetings parents who fail to raise their children properly.

Struggle against survivals of the past: religious prejudice, drunkenness and hooliganism.

Take measures to strengthen the family, have an influence on those with poor morals, who incorrectly conduct themselves in daily life" '

(A. S. Stoyankina, 1962) p.8.

APPENDIX 4

Table 8: The Location, Pattern of Growth and Extent of the Zhensovety 1949-1981[1]

Date	Republic	Oblast'/Krai	Gorod	Raion	Number Zhensovety	Activists	Reference	
1949	Ukraine						Koval'	(1961)
1955	RSFSR						Borisova	(1956)
1957	RSRSR	Sverdlovskaya	Simferopl'				Kazantseva	(1958)
	RSFSR	Sverdlovskaya	Alapaevsk		13		Buzonov/Popova	(1963)
1958	RSFSR	Altaiskii Krai	Alapaevsk				Brashnikova	(1961)
	RSFSR						Tallya	(1971)
	Uzbekistan	Bukharskaya	Bukharovsk	Bukharskii			1st Uzbek Women's Congress	(1958)
1959	Lithuania		Sheduva	Sheduvskii			Dobrodzeene	(1961)
	RSFSR		Magnitke	Kuzinskii		750	Kuznetsova ed.	(1961)
	RSFSR	Sverdlovskaya			100		Kuriedov	(1959)
	Turkmenistan						Karryeva	(1969)

1. The tabulation is incomplete owing to the lack of systematic Soviet data. It has been compiled from sources used on the zhensovety to give an indication of the extent of reference to individual localities at different periods. No references have been found of zhensovety in the republics of Estonia, Georgia and Armenia. Apart from the RSFSR, there are most references to the Ukraine, followed by Kazhakstan, Moldavia and Turkmenia. Zhensovety are also recorded in ten autonomous republics.

APPENDIX 4: Table 8 contd.

Date	Republic	Oblast'/Krai	Gorod	Raion	Number Zhensovety Activists		Reference
1960	Buryat ASSR			Khorinskii	47		Buryat ASSR Women's Congress (1961)
	Buryat ASSR			Dzhidinskii	29	244	Buryat ASSR Women's Congress (1961)
	Mordovia ASSR				363		Dorozhkin ed. (1967)
	Turkmenia				800		Annanurova (1968)
	Ukraine	Stalino-Donbass	Slavyansk	Slavyanskii	38		Koldova ed. (1961)
	Uzbekistan		Tashkent		1,145		Aminova (1977)
	RSFSR	Leningradskaya	Viborg	Lomonovskii Smolmyskii Vsevolozhskii			Saphozhnikov (1962)
1961	RSFSR	Sverdlovskaya	Alapaevsk	Alapaevskii	40		Popova/Buzonov eds. (1963)
	Central Asia						Shitarev (1961)
	Daghestan						Daghestan 8th Women's Congress (1961)
	Lithuania		Sheduva	Radvilishskii	10		Dobrodzeene (1961)
	Mordavia ASSR		(Saransk)		365		Dorozhkin ed. (1967)
	Moldavia			Tarakliiskii			Sibrayeva (1961)
	RSFSR	Bryanskaya	Suzetke	Suzemskii	24		Kuznetsova (1962)
	RSFSR	Chelyabinskaya	Chelyabinsk		11		Kuznetsova ed. (1961)

APPENDIX 4: Table 8 contd.

Date	Republic	Oblast'/Krai	Gorod	Raion	Number Zhensovety Activists		Reference
1961 contd.		Chelyabinskaya	Miass	Oktyabr'skii	21		Kuznetsova ed. (1961)
	RSFSR	Ul'yanovskaya		Stalinskii	700		Polegeshko (1961)
	RSFSR	Ul'yanovskaya		Kuzovalevskii	40		Polegeshko (1961)
	Ukraine	Donetskaya	Gorkovka	Barishskii			Koldova ed. (1961)
	Ukraine	Stalino-Donbass		Artemovskii			Koldova ed. (1961)
	Ukraine	Zaporozhskaya	Zaporozhe		1		Koldova ed. (1961)
	Uzbekistan				5,613	30,000	Uzbekistan 2nd Women's Congress (1961)
1962	Daghestan						El'darova (1963)
	RSFSR	Kharkovskaya			977	8,965	Maneshin (1962)
	RSFSR	Sverdlovskaya	Berezovka	Berezovskii			Stoyankina (1962)
	RSFSR	Kaliningradskaya		Goritskii			Stoyankina (1962)
	RSFSR	Ul'yanovskaya	Barish	Barishskii			Stoyankina (1962)
	RSFSR	Orlovskaya					Stoyankina (1962)
	RSFSR		Saratov.	Zavod			Belyaeva (1962)
1964	Latvia				404	3,083	Lozinski (1964)
	Mordovia				500+		Dorozhkin ed. (1967)
	Ukraine				500		Polishchuk ed. (1964)
	Uzbekistan				5,700		Nasriddinova (1964)
					5,760	93,000	Bol'shaya Sovetskaya Entsiklopediya (1972)

APPENDIX 4: Table 8 contd.

Date	Republic	Oblast'/Krai	Gorod	Raion	Number Zhensovety	Reference
1965	Kazhakstan				9,000	*Rabotnitsa* staff member (7.1.81)
	Tadzhikistan		Dushanbe	Oktyabr	50	Zaripova (1965)
	Ukraine				4,000	*Rabotnitsa* staff member (7.1.81)
1968	Daghestan					Gasenbekova (1979)
	Turkmenia					Annanurova (1968)
1969	Chuvash				1,657	Tallya (1971)
	Mari ASSR				589	Tallya (1971)
	Mordovia ASSR				675	Tallya (1971)
	Turkmenia				800	Ashkhabad conference (1972)
	Yakutia ASSR				1,000	Yakutia—5th Women's Congress (1969)
1970	Kazhakstan				4,175	Ashkhabad conference (1972)
1971	Uzbekistan	Kashkadar'inskaya		Skakhrisabzskii		Babadzhanova (1971)
1973	Turkmenia		Ashkhabad	Ashkhabadskii	7	Myatieva (1973)
1974	Chuvash				1,600	Tallya (1975)
1975	Belorussia	Vitebskaya		Liozonskii		*Krest'yanka* No. 7 (1975)
	Daghestan				1,000	Gasenbekova (1979)

APPENDIX 4: Table 8 contd.

Date	Republic	Oblast'/Krai	Gorod	Raion	Number Zhensovety	Reference	
1975 contd.	Lithuania				4,000	Dirzhinskaiete	(1975)
	Mari ASSR				100	Prosvetova et. al	(1975)
	Moldavia					Vartik	(1975)
	RSFSR		Ivanovo			Ivanovno Plenum	(1975)
	RSFSR	Rostovskaya		Lipetskii		Krest'yanka, No. 10	(1975)
	RSFSR			Azobskii		Krest'yanka, No. 2	(1975)
1976	Kazhakstan	Alma-Atinskaya	Talgar	Iliiskii		Krest'yanka, No. 3	(1976)
	Kirghizia			Uzgenskii		Krest'yanka, No. 8	(1976)
	Moldavia			Edinetskii		Rotar'	(1976)
	RSFSR	Belgorodskaya		Belgorodskii		Cheidene	(1980)
	RSFSR	Kalinin				Krest'yanka, No. 9	(1976)
	RSFSR	Khakasskaya auton oblast'					
	RSFSR	Krasnoyarski krai				Krest'yanka, No. 3	(1976)
	RSFSR	Lipetskaya		Lipetskii		Krest'yanka, No. 9	(1976)
	RSFSR	Oshskaya		Uzgenskii		Krest'yanka, No. 8	(1976)
	Tadzhikistan			Regarskii	28	Krest'yanka, No. 10	(1977)
1977	RSFSR	Karsnoyarskii krai				Belenkii and Rakhimov	(1978)
	RSFSR			Krasnodarsk		Krest'yanka, No. 11	(1977)
	RSFSR	Tul'skaya		Uzlovskii		Krest'yanka, No. 4	(1977)

APPENDIX 4: Table 8 contd.

Date	Republic	Oblast'/Krai	Gorod	Raion	Number Zhensovety	Reference
1978	Chuvash		Slavgaskurot		1,700	*Krest'yanka*, No. 11 (1978)
	Moldavia				2,000	*Krest'yanka*, No. 10 (1978)
	Moldavia			Chmishliiskii & Sorokskii		*Krest'yanka*, No. 10 (1978)
	Moldavia			Slobodzelskii	820	*Krest'yanka*, No. 10 (1978)
	Moldavia			Strashenskii		*Krest'yanka*, No. 10 (1977)
	Mari					Moshunova (1978)
	RSFSR	Novosibirsk	Bersk			Cheidene (1980)
	RSFSR	Rostovskaya		Salskii		*Krest'yanka*, No. 1 (1978)
	Tadzhikistan			Pamir	114	*Krest'yanka*, No. 2 (1978)
	Turkmenia		Tashau	Tashauskii		Mollaeva (1978)
	Ukraine	Karkovskaya		Valkovskii		Fomina (1978)
	Ukraine	Khersonskaya	Kherson			*Krest'yanka*, No. 12 (1978)
	Ukraine	Zaporozhskaya	Zaporozhe			*Krest'yanka*, No. 3 (1978)
1979	Kazhakstan	Kokchekavskaya				*Krest'yanka*, No. 11 (1979)
	RSFSR	Krasnoyarsk krai		Tokmakskii	18,000	*Krest'yanka*, No. 1 (1980)
1980	Azerbaidjan					Zhvirble (1980)
	Baltic Republics					Zhvirble (1980)
	Belorussia					Moskvina (1980)
	Checheno-Ingush ASSR					*Krest'yanka*, No. 9 (1980)

APPENDIX 4: Table 8 contd.

Date	Republic	Oblast'/Krai	Gorod	Raion	Number Zhensovety	Reference	
1980 contd.	Chuvash						
	Karelia ASSR					Krest'yanka, No. 12	(1980)
	Kazhakstan					Zhvirble	(1980)
	Kazhakstan	Kokchetavskaya		Kokchetavskii		Boleiko	(1980)
	Kirghizia					Sovetskaya Kultura	(8.3.80)
						Sovetskaya Kirghizia	(8.3.80)
	Lithuania					Sovetskaya Litva	(8.3.80)
	Mari ASSR					Krest'yanka, No. 12	(1980)
	Moldavia					Moskvina	(1980)
	RSFSR	Altaiskii krai				Krest'yanka, No. 1	(1981)
	RSFSR	Irkutskaya	Tulin	Tulinskii		Krest'yanka, No. 8	(1980)
	RSFSR	Irkutskaya		43 town/raion 600 enterprise		Zhvirble	(1980)
	RSFSR	Novogorodskaya		Batetskii		Krest'yanka, No. 1	(1980)
	RSFSR	Omskaya				Krest'yanka, No. 11	(1980)
	Tadzhikistan				1,310	Bobosadykova	(1980)
	Turkmenia					Zhvirble	(1980)
	Tuvinskaya ASSR					Krest'yanka, No. 3	(1980)
	Ukraine					Moskvina	(1980)
	Ukraine	Vinnitskaya		Yampol'skii		Krest'yanka, No. 10	(1980)

APPENDIX 4: Table 8 contd.

Date	Republic	Oblast'/Krai	Gorod	Raion	Number Zhensovety Activists	Reference	
1981	Bashkiriya ASSR			Sterlibashevskii		*Krest'yanka*, No. 9	(1981)
	Belorussia	Brestskaya		Drogichinskii		*Krest'yanka*, No. 4	(1981)
	Komi ASSR					Chuprova	(1981)
	Moldavia					*Krest'yanka*, No. 2	(1981)
	RSFSR	Altaiskii Krai		Smolenskii		*Krest'yanka*, No. 7	(1981)
	RSFSR	Lipetskaya		Dobrinskii		*Krest'yanka*, No. 1	(1981)
				Dobrovskii			
				Gryazinskii			
				Lipetskii			
				Uzmanskii			
	RSFSR	Rostovskaya				Imamova	(1981)
	RSFSR				82	*Krest'yanka*, No. 2	(1981)
	RSFSR	Trimorskii Krai			1,000	Mishchenko	(1981)

Selected Bibliography

SOVIET SOURCES
(excluding titles listed under Womens Congresses and Soviet Dissertations)

Abramova, A. F. (1978), *Okhrana Truda Zhenshchin* (Spravochnik po zakonodatel'stvu) (Moscow, Profizdat).

Aleekseva, G. N. (1963), *Programma KPSS—yarkoe proyavlenie zabot' partii o zhenshchinakh* (Tashkent, Tashkent ob'edin.).

Alexandrova, T. (1975), 'Why Soviet Women Want to Work', *New Times*, No. 10, pp.20-2.

Alkhazova, A. P. (1964), *Dela Zhensoveta* (Makhachkala, Dagkingoizdat).

Aminova, R. Kh. (1977), *The October Revolution and Women's Liberation in Uzbekistan* (Moscow, Nauka).

Annanurova, C. (1968), 'Massovaya rabota sredi zhenshchin-turkmenok', *Politicheskoe Samobrazie*, No. 3, pp.113-15.

Ashkhabad conference, *Ozvobozhdenaya Zhenshchina Sovetskovo Vostoka* (1972), (material from inter-republic conference, Ashkhabad 26-27 Oct. 1970) (Ashkhabad, 'Turkmenistan').

Babadzhanova, R. N. (1971), *Partiei 'Vdokhnovlennye'* (Deyatel'nost; partiinykh organizatsii Uzbekistana po usileniyu aktivnosti zhenshchin v Kommunisticheskoi stroitel'stve) (Tashkent, 'Uzbekistan').

Baskina, Ada (1979), *About Women Like Me: Public and Private Life in the USSR* (Moscow, Novosti).

Belenkii, V. Kh. and Rakhimov, A. R. (1978), 'Current Problems in the Study of Socialist Democracy', *Soviet Sociology*, Vol. LXVII, No. 1, pp.83-101.

Belyaeva, A. S. (1962), *Zhenskie Sovety* (Saratov).

Bil'shai Vera (1958), 'Sotsializma i Emansipatsiya Zhenshchin', *Kommunist*, No. 3, pp.40-1.
Biryukova, A. P. ed. (1979), *Komissiya po rabote sredi zhenshchin pri FZMK (Moscow, Profizdat)*.
Biryukova, Alexandra (1980), 'For the Working Mother', *Soviet Woman*, No. 7, p.3.
Biryukova, Alexandra (1985), 'The Role of the Soviet Woman in Decision-making in Trade Union Committees and in Industry', *Labour and Society*, Vol. LX, No. 3, pp.307-21.
Bobosadykova, G. B. (1979), *Zhenshchina-activnyi stroitel' Kommunizma* (Dushanbe, Tsk. K. P. Tadzhikistan otdel.).
Bobosadykova, G. B. (1980), 'Tochka Otscheta', *Rabotnitsa*, No. 11, pp.7-9.
Bochkareva, E. I. and Lyubimova, S. T. (1967), *Sveltyi put': Kommunisticheskaya Partiia Sovetskovo Soyuza—borets za svobodu, ravnopravie i shchast'e zhenshchiny* (Moscow, Profizdat).
Bochkaryova, E. and Lyubimova, S. (1969), *Women of a New World* (Moscow, Progress).
Boiko, V. I. (1965), 'Sochetanie gosudarstvennykh i obshchestvennykh nachal v deyatel'nosti mestnykh sovetov', in P. S. Cheremnykh ed. (1965).
Bol'shaya Sovetskaya Entsiklopediya (1972) Vol. 9, 3rd edn (Moscow).
Boleiko, L. (1980), 'V Opore na Aktiv', *Partiinaya Zhizn Kazakstana*, No. 2, pp.36-40.
Borisova, N. A. (1956), *Zhenskii Sovet* (Simferopl', Krymizdat).
Brashnikova, E. F. (1961), *Zhenskie Sovety na Altae* (Barnaul, Altknig).
Buzonov, V. E. and Popova, Z. S., eds. (1963), *Zhenshchiny Urala v Revolutsii i Trude* (Sverdlovsk, Sverdlovskoe knizhnoe izdatel'stvo).

Cheremnykh, N. I. ed. (1964), *Sily v nikh kroyutsa neischislimye: O rabote zhenskikh sovetov g. Chelyabinska* (Chelyabinsk, Yuzn.-Uralskoe kniznoe izdatel'stvo).
Chkhikvadze, V. M., ed. (1965), *Sotsialism i Narodovlastie* (spravochnik) (Moscow, Politicheskaya Literatura).
Chuprova, L. (1981), 'Zhivem v pripolya're', *Krest'yanka*, No. 6, p.10.

Dakhimbabaeva, Z. (1958), 'Uzbekskie Zhenshchina—aktivnye stroiteli Kommunizma', *Kommunist*, No. 9, pp.51-60.
Danilov, Leonid (1981), *11th Five Year Plan: The Soviet Union*

Today and Tomorrow (Moscow, Novosti).
Danilova, Y. Z. *et al.* (1975), *Soviet Women (Some aspects of the status of women in the USSR)* (Moscow, Progress).
Darchieva, N. K. (1975), 'Kritika nekotorykh burzhuaznykh fal'sifikatsii polozheniya zhenshchiny v SSSR', *Nauchnii Kommunizma*, No. 6, pp.105-11.
Dirzhinskaiete, L. (1975a), 'Sovetskaya Zhenshchina—Aktivnyi stroitel' Kommunizma', *Partiinaya Zhizn*, No. 20, p.28.
Dirzhinskaiete, L. (1975b), *Sovetskaya Litva*, (27 April) p.2.
Dobrodzeene, A. (1961), 'Slovo-zhenshchinam', *Kommunist Latvii*, No. 2, pp.48-50.
Dorozhkin, M. V. *et al.* (1967), *Ocherki istorii Mordovskii organizatsii KPSS* (Saransk, Kafedra Istorii KPSS Mordov).

Efimov, Mikhail (1979), *APN Comments on the USSR Constitution* (Moscow, Novosti Press Agency Publishing House).
Egorova, N. A. (1976), *Zhenshchina v Sovremennom Mire* (Erevan, Aistan).
El'darova, R. A. (1963), *Zhenshchiny Gor: Politicheskaya rabota sredi zhenshchin Dagestana* (Makhachkala, Dagknig).
Eremeeva, R. G. (1981), *O Zhenshchinakh—Zabota Osbaya* (Moscow, Moskovskii Rabochii).
Esieva, F. B. and Shilova, G. F. eds. (1980), *XXV S'ezd Kommunisticheskoi Partii Sovetskovo Soyuza o Roli Zhenshchin v Razvitom Sotsialisticheskom Obshchestve* (iz opyta raboty partiinoi organizatsii Perovskaya raiona g. Moskva) (Moscow, Akademiya Obshchestvennikh Nauk pri Tsk. KPSS).

Fomina, M. (1978), 'Dlya Lyudei', *Krest'yanka*, No. 6, pp.18-19.

Golubeva, V. N. (1981), speech to 26th Congress CPSU, *Pravda* (25 Jan.) pp.4-5.
Groshev, I. I., ed. (1980), *Deyatel'nost' KPSS po povysheniyu roli zhenshchin stroitel'stve Kommunizma* (sbornik statei) (Moscow, Akademiya Obshchestvennikh Nauk).
Gurtovnik, M. (1963), 'Zhensovet Alapaevska za rabotoi', in V. E. Buzonov and Z. S. Popova, eds. (1963).

Il'icheva, L. (1959), 'Voprosy kommunisticheskovo vospitaniya trudyashchikhsya', *Kommunist*, No. 41, p.47.
Imamova, V. (1981), 'Zhenshchiny Doma-Pyatiletke', *Rabotnitsa*, No. 7, pp.20-1.

Kadeikan, V. A. *et al.* (1974), *Voprosy vnutripartiinoi zhizni i rukovdyashchei deyatel'nosti KPSS na sovremennom etape* (Moscow, Mysl').

Kardashin, L. and Kalishevski, V. (1977), 'Zhenshchiny iz Korenovki', *Krest'yanka*, No. 11, pp.26-7.

Kazantseva, E. (1958), 'Chto daet differentsirovannaya rabota s lyudmi', *Partiinaya Zhizn*, No. 13, pp.44-7.

Khasanova, N. (1977), 'S Rodnoi Partiei', *Krest'yanka*, No. 10, p.4.

Khosyaiskii Zhenskikh Glag (1961) (Sbornik statei zhensovetov) (Simferopol', Krymizdat).

Khvorostyani, N. (1960), 'Navstrechu XX1oi S'ezd K. P. Ukrainy, sovreshenstvat' i rasirostranyat' luchshie formy politicheskoi raboty v massakh', *Kommunist Ukrainy*, No. 1, pp.32-7.

Koldova, V. I. ed. (1961), *Zabotlivye Ruki: iz opyta raboty zhenskikh sovetov* (Stalino-Donbass, otdel' partiinykh organov Stalinskovo obkoma K. P. Ukrainy).

Kolesnikov, A. K. (1958), *Organizatorskaya deyatel'nost' KPSS v massakh* (Moscow, Znanie).

Kollontai, Alexandra (1972), *Sexual Relations and the Class Struggle* (Bristol, Falling Wall Press).

Kollontai, Alexandra (1977), *Selected Writings*, ed. and trans. Alix Holt (London, Allison & Busby).

Komitet Sovetskikh Zhenshchin (1978), *Rol' Sovetskikh zhenshchin v gosudarstvenny upravlenii i v obshchestvenno-politicheskoi zhizni strany* (Moscow, Novsti).

Kon, Igor, (1975), 'Women at Work: Equality with a Difference?', *International Social Science Journal*, Vol. XXVII, No. 4.

Kondrenikov, A. A. (1976), *Klyuchevoe Zveno Partiinovo Rukovodstva* (Moscow).

Konukhovskii, V. N. and Ovlyannikov, N. M. (1960), '21ii S'ezd KPSS o politicheskoi zadachakh partii v period osushchestvleniya semiletnovo plana', *Znanie Vsesoyuznoe Obshchestvo*, No. 23, pp.17-28.

Kotelenetz, A. I. (1977), *Zhenshchiny Strany Sovetov* (Moscow, Politizdat).

Koval', N. A. (1961), *Podrugi Moryakov* (Moscow, Morskoi Transport).

Krasil'shchikova, S. A. (1975), 'Zhenshchiny v mezhdunarodnom dvizhenii za mir i sotsial'noi progress', *Vestnik Akademii Nauk SSSR*, Vol. XLV, part 11, pp.126-8.

Krupskaya, N. K. (1937), *Soviet Woman: A Citizen with Equal Rights. A collection of articles and speeches* (Moscow, Co-operative Publishing Society of Foreign Workers in the USSR).

Kuriedov, V. (1959), 'Po-delovomu rukovodit' massovo-politicheskoi rabotoi', *Partiinaya Zhizn*, No. 9, pp.14-18.

Kuroglo, S. S. and Filimonova, M. F. (1976), *Proshloe i Nastoyashchee Gagauzskoi Zhenshchiny* (Kishinev, Kartya Moldovenskaya).
Kuznetsova, K. P. ed. (1961), *Zabotlivye ruki, shchedrye serdtsa. O rabota zhenskikh sovetov Chelyabinska* (Chelyabinsk).
Kuznetsova, Larissa (1979), 'Adam, Eva i vek-iskustel'', *Literaturnaya Gazetta*, No. 1 (1 Jan).
Kuznetsova, M. S. (1962), *Est' v Suzemke Zhensovet* (Bryansk, Buyanskii rabochii).

Lekovitch, M. V. et al. (1975), *Bez nikh my ne pobedili by* (Moscow, Politizdat).
Lenin, V. I. (1944), 'What is to be Done?', in *Selected Works, Vol. 2, The Struggle for the Bolshevik Party (1900-1904)* (London, Lawrence and Wishart).
Lenin, V. I. (1977), *On the Emancipation of Women* (Moscow, Progress).
Levin, B. and Levin, M. (1978), 'Women's Drinking', *Literaturnaya Gazetta*, (20 Dec.) p.12, condensed in *Current Digest of the Soviet Press (CDSP)*, Vol. XXXI, No. 3, pp.5-6.
Litvinova, G. I. and Popova, N. V. (1975), 'Istoricheskii opyt resheniya zhenskovo voprosa v SSSR', *Voprosy Istorii*, No. 11, pp.3-18.
Lozinski, Z. (1964), 'K obshchestvennomu kommunisticheskomu samoupravlenniyu', in *Silami Obshchestvennosti* (Sbornik statei ob uchastii obshchestvennosti v rabote sovetskikh organov) (Riga, Latgosizdat).
Luchat', Y. ed. (1958), 'Rabotu s Kardrami (s partiinikh konferensov i kongresov)', *Partiinaya Zhizn*, No. 5, pp.45-7.
Lukin, A. (1981), 'L'goty dlya zhenshchin', *Krest'yanka*, No. 3, p.29.
Lyubimova, S. T. (1969), 'Detatel'nosti Zhenotdelov', *Voprosy Istorii KPSS*, No. 9, pp.68-77.

Makeeva, N. (1961), 'Kak postavleno partiino rukovodstvo zhenskikh sovetakh v Slavyanske', in V. I. Koldova ed. (1961).
Maneshin, V. S. (1962), *Obshchestvennye Organizatsii Trudyashchikhsya*, (Kharkov).
Mel'nikova, N. (1961), 'Entusiastiki', in V. I. Koldova ed. (1961) pp.50-2.
Mishchenko, P. (1981), 'Izo Dnya v Den'', *Rabotnitsa*, No. 7, pp.20-1.
Mitskevich, A. V. (1959), 'Rashirenie roli obshchestvennykh organizatsii v period razvernutovo stroitel'stva Kommunizma',

Sovetskoe Gosudarstvo i Pravo, No. 9, pp.24-33.
Mollaeva, M. (1978), 'Rastet Sotsial'naya Aktivnost' Sovetskikh Zhenshchin', *Partiinaya Zhizn*, No. 5, pp.57-62.
Musakhanova, M. (1966), 'Politicheskaya rabota sredi zhenshchin Uzbekistana *Politicheskoe Samoobrazovanie*, No. 3, pp.102-7.
Moshunova, V. (1978), 'Glavnaya Zadacha', *Krest'yanka*, No. 3, p.14.
Moskvina, M. (1980-1), *Correspondence*, Soviet women's committee.
Muzyrya, M. (1980), 'Vse Sbyvaetsya . . .', *Sovetskaya Zhenshchina*, No. 10.
Myatieva, A. (1973), *Dela i Dumy Zhenshchin* (iz opyta raboty zhensoveta shveinoi fabriki No. 2, gorod Ashkhabada) (Ashkhabad, 'Turkmenistan').

Nasriddinova, Y. S. (1964), *Zhenshchiny Uzbekistana* (Tashkent, 'Uzbekistan').
Neshcheretnii, P. (1980), 'Chlenstvo v Partii—Povyshenie zvaniya Kommunista', *Partiinaya Zhizn*, No. 4, pp.19-25.
Nikolaeva-Tereshkova, V. V. (1975a), 'Status of Women in Soviet Society', *Convergence*, Vol. VIII, No. 1, pp.34-7.
Nikolaeva-Tereshkova, V. V. (1975b), 'The Woman Question in Contemporary Soviet Life', *Pravda* (4 March), trans. *CDSP*, Vol. XXVII, No. 9, pp.1-2.
Nikolaeva-Tereshkova, V. V. (1980), 'Soviet Women Building Communism', in *Women in Socialist Society* (Moscow, CMEA) pp.46-60.
Novikova, Y. E., Yazykova, V. S., Yankova, Z. A. (1978), *Zhenshchina, Trud, Sem'ya (Sotsiologicheskii ocherk)* (Moscow, Profizdat).
Novikova, Y. E. (1980), 'The USSR', in *Work and Family Life: The role of the social infrastructure of Eastern European countries* (Geneva, International Labour Office) pp.61-70.

Ostapenko, L. V. (1980), 'The Effect of Women's New Production Role on her Position in the Family', trans. in *Soviet Sociology*, Vol. XII, (Spring) pp.85-99.
Otchizna (1981), 'Ne po Dolgy a po Sovesti' (March), pp.4-6.
Ozvobozhdenaya Zhenshchina Sovetskovo Vostoka (1972), (material from inter-republic conference, Ashkhabad 26-27 Oct. 1970) (Ashkhabad, 'Turkmenistan').

Pankratova, A. M. (1956), *Sovetskie zhenshchiny imeyut ravnye politicheskie prava s muzhinami, i aktivna uchastvuyut v*

upravlenii gosudarstvom (Moscow).
Pavlova, K. L. and Chernyadeva, I. (1961), 'Khozyaiki Bol'shovo Goroda', in K. P. Kuznetsova ed. (1961).
Pimenova, A. L. (1971), 'Novi byt i stanovlenie vnutrisemeinovo raventsva', *Sotsial'nye Issledovaniya*, No. 7, pp.34-45.
Polegeshko, A. P. (1961), *Nashi Aktivistki (Rabota zhensoveta kolkhozov, sovkhozov, i prom. predpriyatii)* (Ul'yanovsk).
Polishchuk, S. P. ed. (1964), *Nashi Aktivistki (Sbornik statei o rabote zhensovetov v Odesse i Izmaile)* (Odessa, Mayak).
Prosvetova, O. V., Nabatohitkova, S. V., Georgina, M. A. (1975) *Zhenshchiny Marinskoi ASSR* (Ioshkar-Ola, Marknigoizdat).
Purvanskaiete, V. (1980), 'Radi, Mira i Shchast'ya', *Sovetskaya Litva*, (8 March). p.2.

Riurikov, Yuri (1977a), 'Deti i Obshchestvo', *Voprosy Filosofi*, No. 4, pp.111-27.
Riurikov, Yuri (1977b), 'Why there are fewer children', *Soviet Sociology*, Vol. XXX, No. 42, pp.6-7.
Rotar', A. A. (1976), 'Opora na Aktiv', *Krest'yanka*, No. 7, pp.22-3.
Rudenko, I. (1978), 'One Time, After a Dance—Polemical Notes About a Strange Weakness of the "Weaker Sex" ', *Komsomolskaya Pravda*, (14 May) p.2. Abstract plus reader's replies trans. *CDSP*, Vol. XXX, No. 42, pp.6-7.
Rusakova, V., Ryabinkina, T., Timofeeva, Z. (1979), 'Bol'she Vsekh Nushno' (conference of 'social' activists organised by *Rabotnitsa*) *Rabotnitsa*, No. 10, pp.4-7.
Rutyantseva, M., Pergament, A, Gramova, G. (1963), *Spravochnik Zhenshchiny Rabotnitsy* (Moscow, Profizdat).

Sapozhnikov, I. N. (1962), *Voprosy Partiinovo Stroitel'stva (Sbornik lektsii opyte raboty partorganizatsii Leningrada i Leningradskaya oblast'* (Leningrad, Lenizdat).
Sedugin, P. (1973), *New Soviet Legislation on Marriage and the Family* (Moscow, Progress).
Sheinina, V. I. (1980), 'Sovet Otsov', *Sovetskaya Zhenshchina*, No. 10, p.28.
Shevtsov, V. (1979), *Citizenship of the USSR (A legal study)* (Moscow, Progress).
Shitarev, G. I. (1959), 'Vozrastanie roli KPSS v period razvernutovo stroitel'stva Kommunizma', *Vsesoyuznoe Obshchestvo*, No. 20.
Shitarev, G. I. (1961), 'O novyvkh formakh partiinoi raboty', *Partiinaya Zhizn*, No. 11, pp.9-16.

Shukorova, Kh. S. (1961), *Kommunisticheskaya Partiya Uzbekistana v bor'be za raskreposhchenie zhenshchin* (Tashkent, Izdatel'stvo Uzbekistana).
Shukurova, Kh. S. ed. (1982), *Kommunisticheskaya Partiya Uzbekistana i rabota sredi zhenshchin Respubliki (1938-58) (Sbornik dokumentov materialov)* (Tashkent, 'Uzbekistan').
Sibrayeva, V. (1961), 'Kak my organisuem vospitatel'nuyu rabotu sredi zhenshchin', *Kommunist Moldavii*, No. 4, pp.42-6.
Sidirova, T. N. (1980), 'Zhenshchina—peredovik proizvodstva professional'naya i bytovaya situatsii', *Sotsialogicheskie Issledovaniya*, No. 1, pp.102-7.
Sidirova, T. N. (1981), *Trud i sovremennaya zhenshchina (opyt sotsiologicheskovo issledovaniya)* (Moscow, Profizdat).
Slaishcheva, N. (1978), 'Konstitutsiya SSSR i Prava Sovetskikh Zhenshchin', *Agitator*, No. 3.
Slaishcheva, N. (1980), 'Zhenshchiny v Sovetakh', *Agitator*, No. 5, pp.26-7.
Solob'ev, N. Ya. (1981), *Sem'ya v Sotsialisticheskom Obshchestve* (Moscow, Izdatel'stvo politicheskoi literatury).
Sonin, M. Ya. (1978), 'Equal Rights, Unequal Burdens', *Ekonomika i organizatsia promyshlennovo proizvodstva*, No. 3, pp.5-18, Abstract trans. *CDSP* Vol. XXX, No. 30, pp.3-4.
Soviet Women's Committee (1975) (Moscow, Novosti).
Stakeeva, A. (1977), *Deyatel'nost' K. P. Kirgizii po usileniyu tvorcheskoi aktivnosti zhenshchin v kommunisticheskom stroitel'stve 1959-65)* (Frunze).
Starodub, V. I. (1975), *Zhenshchina i Obshchestvennyi Trud* (Leningrad, Lenizdat).
Stoyankina, A. S. (1962), *Zhenskie Sovety* (Moscow, Sovetskaya Rossiya).
Strepuhov, M. (1965), Razvitie sotsialisticheskoi demokratii', *Agitator*, No. 2, pp.12-15.

Tallya, O. I. (1975), *Politicheskaya Rabota Sredi Zhenshchin (iz opyta partiinykh organizatsii i zhenskikh sovetov Chuvashskoi ASSR* (Cheboksary, Chuvashskoe knizhnoe izdatel'stvo).
Tatarinova, N. (1958), 'Zhenskii trud v narodny khozyaistve SSSR', *Kommunist*, No. 16, p.68.
Tatarinova, N. (1968), *Women in the USSR* (Moscow, Novosti).
Tatybekova, Zh. S. (1967), *Zhenshchiny Sovetskovo Kirgizstana v bor'be za sotsializma i kommunizm* (Frunze).
Tatybekova, Zh. S. ed. (1976), *1938-58 Uchastie zhenshchin Kirgizii v stoitel'stve sotsializma* (Frunze, 'Kyrgyzatan').
Titarenko, S. L. (1971), 'Modern Times and Lenin's Teaching of

the Party', in *Development of Revolutionary Theory by the CPSU* (1971) (Moscow, Progress) pp.168-204.
Toshchakova, E. M. (1973), *Zhenshchina v obshchestve i sem'e i sovremennykh almaitsev* (Novosibirsk, Nauka).

Varchuk, V. V. and Razin, V. I. (1967), 'Issledovaniya v oblasti politicheskoi organizatsii sotsialisticheskovo obshchestva', *Voprosy Filosofi*, No. 4, pp.134-43.
Vartik, V. (1975), 'Zabota i eshche raz zabota', *Krest'yanka*, No. 7.

The Woman Question, Selection from the writings of Karl Marx, Frederick Engels, Joseph Stalin (1951) (New York, International Publishers).
Women in Eastern Europe Group ed. (1980), *Women and Russia. First Feminist Samizdat* trans. Women in Eastern Europe Group (London, Sheba Feminist Publishers).

Yakimenko, Nina (1961), 'Discussion of Draft of Party Programme 1961', trans. *CDSP*, Vol. XIII, No. 32, pp.23-4.
Yakolev, Dr. (1978), 'Crime as a Social-legal Phenomenon', trans. *CDSP*, Vol. XXX, No. 1, p.14.
Yankova, Z. A. (1970), O semeino-bytovykh roliakh rabotaiyushchei zhenshchiny', *Sotsial'nye Issledovaniya*, No. 4, pp.76-87.
Yankova, Z. A. (1974), 'Struktura gorodskoi sem'i v sotsialisticheskom obshchestve', *Sotsialogicheskie Issledovaniya*, No. 1, pp.101-110.
Yankova, Z. A. (1975), 'Razvitie lichnosti zhenshchiny v Sovetskoi obshchestve', *Sotsiologicheskie Issledovaniya*, No. 4, pp.42-45.
Yankova, Z. A. (1978), *Sovetskaya Zhenshchina: Sotsial'nyi portret* (Moscow, Politizdat).
Yatrol'skaya, Ts. A. (1972), *Obshchestvennie organizatsii v SSSR* (Moscow, Nauka).
Yemelyanova, Y. D. (1975), 'The Social and Political Acitivity of Women', in Y. Z. Danilova *et al.* (1975).

Zaripova, N. (1965), 'Zhenshchiny—Aktivnie stroiteli kommunizma', *Kommunist*, No. 12. pp.26-33.
Zel'dich, K. (1961), 'Dveri otkryty nastezh', in K. P. Kuznetsova ed. (1961).
Zhenshchina—aktivnyi stroitel' kommunizma, (zonal'nye seminary soveshaniya predstavitelei zhensovetov (1979) (25 Jan.-9 Feb.) (Dushanbe, Ts. K. P. Tadzhikistana, otdel propagandy i agitatsii).

Zhenskikh sovety za rabotoi (Sbornik statei) (1962), (Saransk, Mordov).

WOMEN'S CONGRESSES: DOCUMENTARY MATERIAL AND REPORTS

Buryat ASSR—1st Congress (8-9 July, 1960): *S'ezd Zhenshchin Buryatskoi ASSR 1i. Materialy s'ezda* (Ulen-ude, 1961).
Chuvash—5th Congress: *Krest'yanka*, No. 11 (1978) pp.22-3.
Daghestan—8th Congress: *Khozyaika strani gor. Materialy raboty 8vo S'ezda Zhenshchin Dagestana* (Makhachkala, 1961).
Kazhakstan—1st Congress (24. July 61): *Pravda*, 25 July 1961.
Komi—7th Congress: Rusakova, V. 'Vuktyl-Ne Tyl', *Rabotnitsa*, No. 1 (1982) pp.11-12.
Krasnoyarsk—3rd krai Congress: *Krest'yanka*, No. 1 (1980) pp.10-11.
Lithuania—4th Congress: 'Bol'shoi Sovet', Barsharina, V., *Rabotnitsa*, No. 2 (1982) p.6.
Mari ASSR—1st Congress: Prosvetova, O. V., *et al.*, *Zhenshchiny Marinskoi ASSR* (Ioshkar-Ola, Marknigoizdat, 1975).
Moldavia—3rd Congress: 'Bol'shaya Obshchestvennaya Sila', *Krest'yanka*, No. 10 (1978) pp.23-4.
Rostovskaya oblast'—6th Congress: Imamova, V., 'Zhenshchiny Doma-Pyatiletke', *Rabotnitsa*, No. 7 (1981) pp.20-1.
Turkmenistan—1st Congress: *S'ezd Zhenshchin Turkmenistane* (Ashkhabad, 1961).
Uzbekistan—1st Congress (7-8 March 1958): *S'ezd Zhenshchin Uzbekistana*, stenograficheski otchet (Tashkent, Gosizdat USR, 1959).
Uzbekistan—2nd Congress (16-17 May 1961): *S'ezd Zhenshchin Uzbekistana*, stenograficheski otchet (Tashkent, Gosizdat USR, 1962).
Yakutia—5th Congress (8-9 April 1969): Arzhakova, K. S., *et al.*, *V Stroyu Edinoi S'ezd Zhenshchin Yakutii 5i* (Yakutsk, 1970).

SOVIET DISSERTATIONS (UNPUBLISHED)

Cheidene, Valentina (1980) 'Deyatel'nost' KPSS po Povysheniyu Roli Zhenshchin v Upravlenii Obshchenarodnym Gosudarstvom' (Moscow, Kafedra Istorii KPSS).
Gasenbekova, M. D. (1979) 'Deyatel'nost' Dagestanskoi

Organizatsii KPSS po Dal'neishemu Povysheniyu Obshchestvenno-politicheskoi i Proizvodstvennoi Aktivnosti Zhenshchin v Usloviyakh i Razvytovo Sotsializma (1966-75)' (Makhachkala, Dagestan State University.
Ismailova, Ya. I. (1975) 'Deyatel'nost' Partiinoi Organizatsii Azerbaidzhana v Oblasti Povysheniya Roli Zhenshchin v Kulturnoi Stroitel'stve 1946-58' (abstract) (Baku).
Kalinina, T. V. (1980) 'Kritika Burzhuaznykh Fal'sifikatsii Deyatel'nosti KPSS Sredi Zhenshchin' (abstract) (Moscow).
Karryeva, R. P. (1969) 'Borba Kommunisticheskoi Partii Turkmenistana za Preodelenie Perezhitkov Feodal'no-baiskovo Otnosheniya k Zhenshchin-Turkmenk 1959-65' (abstract) (Ashkhabad, Turkmenistan State University).
Marchuk, A. (1980) 'Sotsial'noe i Pravoe Ravenstvo v Sotsialisticheskom Obshchestve: analiz ravenstva i ravnopraviya zhenshchin i muzhchin' (abstract) (Moscow).
Otke, N. P. (1980) 'Opyt KPSS v Reshenii Zhenskovo Voprosa v Usloviyakh Mnogonatsiyu Sotsialisticheskovo Gosudarstva', (abstract) (Moscow).
Tallya, Ol'ga, Ivanovna (1971) 'Deyatel'nost' KPSS po Povysheniyu Ideino-Politicheskovo Urovnya Sovetskikh Zhenshchin v Usloviyakh Stroitel'stva Kommunizma' (Moscow, Kafedra Istorii, Akademiya Obshchestvennikh Nauk, pri TsK KPSS).
Zhuravleva, V. A. (1980) 'KPSS Organizator Tvorcheskovo Uchastya Zhenshchin v Sozdanii Material' no-tekhnicheskoi Bazy Kommunizma' (abstract) (Moscow).
Zhvirble, S. Ya. (1980) 'Zhenshchiny v Sostave KPSS i ikh Uchastie vo Vnutripartiinoi Zhizni' (Moscow, Kafedra Istorii, Akademiya Obshchestvennikh Nauk, pri Tsk KPSS).

NON-SOVIET SOURCES

Ahrland, Karin (1978) ' "The Obligatory Woman" in Committee Life', *International Journal of Sociology*, Vol. VIII, No. 3.
Albrektsen, Beatrice Halsaa (1978) 'Women's Political Activity', *International Journal of Sociology*, Vol. VIII, No. 3.
Atkinson, Dorothy, Dallin, Alexander, and Lapidus, Gail Warshofsky eds. (1978) *Women in Russia* (Sussex, Harvester Press).
Attwood, Lynne (1985) 'The New Soviet Man and Woman— Soviet Views on Psychological Sex Differences', in Barbara Holland ed. (1985) pp.54-77.
Azmon, Yael (1981) 'Sex, power and authority', *British Journal of*

Sociology, Vol. XXXII, No. 4, pp.547-59.

Barrett, Michele (1980) *Women's Oppression Today, Problems in Marxist Feminist Analysis* (London, Verso).
Beauvoir, Simone de (1953) *The Second Sex* (London, 4 Square).
Bebel, Auguste (1975) *Women Under Socialism* (New York, Schocken).
Beechey, Veronica (1979) 'On Patriarchy', *Feminist Review*, No. 3.
Beltsky, Sergei, Knovalov, Valerii and Krauss, Herwig (1986) 'The CPSU CC full members elected by the 27th Party Congress in March', *Radio Liberty* (RL. 145/86) No. 15.
Bernard, Jessie (1973) 'Adjusting the Lives of Women to the Establishment' in C. S. Stoll ed. *Sexism: Scientific Debates* (Reading Mass., Addison Wesley).
Bialer, Selweryn (1980) *Stalin's Successors: Leadership, stability and change in the Soviet Union* (Cambridge, Cambridge University Press).
Blekher, Feiga (1979) *The Soviet woman in Family and Society (A sociological study)* (Jerusalem, Kater Press Enterprises).
Bobroff, Anne (1976) 'The Bolsheviks and Working Women. 1905-1920', *Radical America*, Vol. X, No. 3, pp.51-73.
Bouchier, D. (1979) 'The Deradicalisation of Feminism: Ideology and Utopia in Action', *Sociology*, Vol. XIII, No. 13, pp.387-402.
Boulding, E. (1977) *Women in the 20th Century World* (New York, John Wiley & Sons).
Bridges, George and Brunt, Rosalind, eds. (1981) *Silver Linings: Some Strategies for the Eighties* (London, Lawrence & Wishart).
Brine, Jenny, Perrie, Maureen and Sutton, Andrew, eds. (1980), *Home, School and Leisure in the Soviet Union* (London, Allen & Unwin).
Brown, A. H. (1974) *Soviet Politics and Political Science* (London, Macmillan).
Brown, Donald, R., ed. (1968) *The Role and Status of Women in the Soviet Union* (New York, Teachers College Press).
Browning, Genia (1977) 'Women, Sexism and Soviet Society', *Socialist Europe* No. 3, pp.14-17.
Browning, Genia (1985) 'Soviet Politics—Where are the Women?' Barbara Holland ed. (1985) pp.207-36.
Browning, Genia K. (1985) 'A consideration of the relationship between the status of women in the USSR and their position in the political leadership, with special reference to the role of Soviet women's groups in raising women's political consciousness' *unpublished dissertation* (London, Polytechnic of the

South Bank).

Bruce, James B. (1976) 'The Politics of Soviet Policy and Khrushchev's Innovative Policies in Education and Agriculture', *Mongraph Series in World Affairs,* Vol. XIII, book 4.

Brunsdon, Charlotte (1978) 'It is well known that by nature women are inclined to be rather personal', *Women Take Issue* (London, Hutchinson) pp. 18-35.

Buckley, Mary (1982) 'Soviet Ideology: The "Woman Question"', paper presented to the annual conference, *National Association for Soviet and East European Studies (27-29 March, 1982).*

Buckley, Mary (1985) 'Soviet Interpretations of the Woman Question' in Barbara Holland, ed., *Soviet Sisterhood* (London, Fourth Estate, 1985) pp.24-53.

Cattell, David (1968) *Leningrad: A case study of Soviet urban government* (New York, Praeger).

Chad, Paul (1977) *Women Under Communism:* Family in Russia and China (New York, Bayside General Hall).

Chetwynd, Jane and Hartnett, Oonagh, eds. (1978) *The Sex Role System: Psychological and Sociological Perspectives* (London, Routledge & Kegan Paul).

Chylinska, Kamila (1968) 'Political Activity of Women in Eastern Europe', *The Annals of the American Academy of Political and Social Science,* Vol. CCCLXXV, pp.67-71.

Ciboski, Kenneth (1972) 'A Woman in Soviet Leadership: Political Career of Madame Furtseva', *Canadian Slavonic Papers, Vol. XIV (Spring) pp.1-14.*

Clark, Lorenne, and Lange, Lynda, eds. (1979) *The Sexism of Social and Political Theory: Women and Reproduction from Plato to Nietzsche* (Toronto, Buffalo, University of Toronto Press).

Clements, Barbara Evans (1980) 'Bolshevik Women: The First Generation', in Toya Yedlin ed., *Women in Eastern Europe and the Soviet Union* (New York, Praeger) pp.65-85.

Cocks, Paul, Daniels, Robert V., and Heer, Nancy Whittier, eds. (1976) *The Dynamics of Soviet Politics* (Cambridge, Mass./London, Harvard University Press).

Comer, Lee (1978) 'The Question of Women and Class', *Women's Studies International Quarterly,* Vol. I, No. 2, pp.165-73.

Conquest, Robert (1967) *The Politics of Ideas in the USSR* (London, Bodley Head).

Constantini, Edmond and Craik, Kenneth (1972) 'Women as Politicians: The Social Background, Personality and Political Careers of Female Party Leaders', *Journal of Social Issues,* Vol.

XXVIII, pp.217-36.
Cook, Blanche Wiesen, ed. (1978) *Chrystal Eastman on Women and Revolution* (New York, Oxford University Press).
Coote, Anna and Campbell, Beatrix (1982) *Sweet Freedom—The Struggle for Women's Liberation* (London, Picador/Pan Books).
Croll, Elizabeth (1978) *Feminism and Socialism in China* (London, Routledge & Kegan Paul).
Currell, Melvill (1974) *Political Woman* (London, Croom Helm).

Davies, Tricia (1981) 'Stand by Your Men? Feminism and Socialism in the Eighties', in George Bridges and Rosalind Brunt eds., *Silver Linings* (London, Lawrence & Wishart).
Delmar, Rosalind (1979) 'Looking again at Engels's *Origin of the Family*', in Juliet Mitchell and Anne Oakley, *Rights and Wrongs of Women* (Harmondsworth, Penguin).
Delphy, Christine (1980) *The Main Enemy: A Materalist Analysis of Women's Oppression* (London, Women's Research and Resources Centre).
Denmark, Florence, L. (1977) 'Styles of Leadership', *Psychology of Women Quarterly*, Vol. II, No. 2, pp.99-113.
Dennis, Michael (1980) 'Women and Political Leadership Positions in the GDR', *GDR Monitor*, No. 3, p.25.
Dobb, Maurice (1970) *Socialist Planning: Some Problems* (London, Lawrence & Wishart).
Dragadze, Tamara (1980) 'A Muslim way of life in the Soviet Union', *New Society* (10 Jan.) pp.56-7.
Drake, Madeline (1980) 'Soviet Child Care: Its Organization at Local Level', in Jenny Brine, Maureen Perrie and Andrew Sutton eds., *Home, School and Leisure in the Soviet Union* (London, Allen & Unwin).
Dunn, Ethel (1978) 'Russian Rural Women', in D. Atkinson *et al.*, *Women in Russia* (Sussex, Harvester Press) pp.167-89.
Duverger, Maurice (1965) *The Political Role of Women* (Paris, UNESCO).

Eisenstein, Zillah, ed. (1979) *Capitalist Patriarchy and the Case for Socialist Feminism* (New York, Monthly Review Press).
Elshtain, Jean Bethke (1974) 'Moral Woman and Immoral Man: A Consideration of the Public-Private Split and its Political Ramifications', *Politics and Society*, Vol. IV, pp.453-73.
Engel, Barbara Alpern (1980) 'Women Revolutionaries: The Personal and the Political', in Toya Yedlin ed., *Women in Eastern Europe and the Soviet Union* (New York, Praeger) pp.31-42.
Engels, Frederick (1977) *The Origin of the Family, Private*

Property and the State (London, Lawrence & Wishart).

Epstein, Cynthia Fuchs, and Coser, Rose Laub, eds. (1980) *Access to Power: Cross National Studies of Women and Elites* (London, Allen & Unwin).

Evans, Mary (1982) 'In praise of theory: the case for women's studies', *Feminist Review*, No. 10, pp.61-74.

Farnsworth, Beatrice Brodsky (1976) 'Bolshevism and the Woman Question', *American Historical Review*, Vol. LXXXI, No. 2, pp.292-316.

Farnsworth, Beatrice Brodsky (1978) 'Bolshevik Alternatives and the Soviet Family: The 1926 Marriage Law Debate', in D. Atkinson *et al.*, *Women in Russia* (Sussex, Harvester Press), pp.139-67.

Ferge, Zsuzsa (1976) 'The Relation between paid and unpaid work of women–a source of inequality, with special reference to Hungary', *Labour and Society*, (April), pp.37-52.

Field, Mark and Flynn, Karin (1970) 'Worker, Mother, Housewife: Soviet Women Today', in Georgene H. Seward and Robert C. Williamson eds., *Sex Roles in Changing Society* (New York, Random House), pp.257-84.

Firestone, Shulamith (1972) *The Dialectic of Sex. The Case for Feminist Revolution* (London, Paladin).

Foverskov, Peter (1978) 'Women in Parliament: sex as a political resource', *European Journal of Political Research*, No. 6, pp.53-69.

Fransella, Fay and Frost, Kay (1977) *On Being a Woman, A Review of Research on how Women see Themselves* (London Tavistock).

Freeman, J. (1974) 'The Politics of the Women's Movement', in Jane Jaquette ed., *Women in Politics* (New York, John Wiley & Sons).

Friedgut, Theodore, H. (1974) 'Community Structure, Political Participation and Soviet Local Government: The Case of Kutaisi', in Henry Walter Morton, and Rudolf Tokes eds., *Soviet Politics and Society in the 1970s* (New York, Free Press).

Friedgut, Theodore, H. (1979) *Political Participation in the USSR* (Princeton, N.J., Princeton University Press).

Garnsey, Elizabeth (1978) 'Women's Work and Theories of Class Stratification', *Sociology*, Vol. XII, No. 12 (May).

Gasiorowska, Zenia (1968) *Women in Soviet Fiction* (Madison, University of Wisconsin Press).

Gehlen, Frieda, L. (1977) 'Women Members of Congress: A

Distinctive Role', in Marianne Githens and Jewel Prestage, A Portrait of Marginality (New York, Longman).
Geiger, Kent (1968) *The Family in Soviet Russia*, Cambridge, Mass., Harvard University Press).
Giele, J. Z., and Smock, A. C., eds. (1977) *Women: Roles and Status in Eight Countries* (New York, John Wiley & Sons).
Githens, Marianne, and Prestage, Jewel, eds. (1977) *A Portrait of Marginality* (New York, Longman).
Gramsci, Antonio (1971) 'State and Civil Society', in Quintin Hoare and Geoffrey Nowell Smith (eds. and trans.) *Selections from the Prison Notebooks of Antonio Gramsci* (London, Lawrence & Wishart).
Greenstein, Fred I. (1961) 'Sex Related Political Differences in Childhood', *Journal of Politics*, No. 2 (May), pp.353-71.

Haavio-Mannila, Elina (1971) 'Convergences between East and West. Tradition and Modern in Sex Roles in Sweden, Finland and the Soviet Union', *Acta-Sociologia*, Vol. XIV, Nos. 1-2, pp.114-23.
Haavio-Mannilla, Elina (1972) 'Sex Roles and Politics', in Constance Safilios-Rothschild, ed., *Toward a Sociology of Women* (Lexington, Mass. Xerox College Publishing), pp.154-72.
Haavio-Mannila, Elina (1978) 'Changes in Sex Roles in Politics as an Indicator of Structural Change in Society, *International Journal of Sociology*, Vol. VIII, No. 3 (Fall), pp.56-85.
Halle, Fanina (1933) *Women in Soviet Russia* (London, Routledge).
Hamilton, Roberta (1978) *The Liberation of Women: Study of Patriarchy and Capitalism* (London, Allen & Unwin).
Hansen, Susan B., Franz, Linda M. and Netemeyer-Mays, Margaret (1976) 'Women's Political Participation and Policy Preferences', Social Science Quarterly, Vol. LVI, No. 4, pp.576-90.
Hansson, Carola and Liden, Karin (1984) *Moscow Women* (London, Allison & Busby).
Harasymiw, Bohdan (1969) 'Nomenklatura: The Soviet Communist Party's Leadership Recruitment System', *Canadian Journal of Political Science* Vol. II, No. 3, pp.493-512.
Harasymiw, Bohdan (1980) 'Have women's chances for political recruitment in the USSR really improved?' in Toya Yedlin, ed., *Women in Eastern Europe and the Soviet Union* (New York, Praeger), pp.140-84.
Heitlinger, Alena (1979) *Women and State Socialism: Sex*

inequality in the Soviet Union and Czechoslovakia (London, Macmillan).

Heitlinger, Alena (1980) 'Marxism, Feminism and Sex Equality', in Toya Yedlin ed., *Women in Eastern Europe and the Soviet Union* (New York, Praeger), pp.9-40.

Heller, Agnes and Vajda, Mihaly (1976) 'Communism and the Family', in A. Hegedus, A. Heller, M. Markus and M. Vajda eds., *The Humanisation of Socialism: Writings of the Budapest School* (London, Allison & Busby), pp.7-26.

Hill, R. J. (1977) *Soviet Political Elites: The Case of Tiraspol* (London, Martin Robertson).

Hill, R. J. and Frank, P. (1981) *The Soviet Communist Party* (London, Allen & Unwin).

Himmelweit, Susan, McKenzie, Margaret and Tomlin, Allison (1978) 'Why Theory?' in *Papers on Patriarchy* (London, PDC and Women's Publishing Collective).

Hoare, Quintin and Smith, Geoffrey Nowell eds. and trans. (1971) *Selections from the Prison Notebooks of Antonio Gramsci* (London, Lawrence & Wishart).

Hoffman, Erik P. (1975) 'The Soviet Union: Consensus or Debate?', *Studies in Comparative Communism,* Vol. VIII, No. 3 (August).

Holland, Barbara, ed. (1985) *Soviet Sisterhood. British Feminists on Women in the USSR* (London, Fourth Estate).

Hollander, Paul, ed. (1969) *American and Soviet Society: A Reader in Comparative Sociology and Perception* (New Jersey, Prentice-Hall).

Hollander, Paul (1973) *Soviet and American Society. A Comparison* (New York, Oxford University Press).

Holt, Alix (1976) 'Women in the Soviet Union. Recent Change: Present Policies and their Implications', unpublished paper, delivered at 'Women in Eastern Europe' Conference (30 Oct.).

Holt, Alix (1977) 'The *Literary Gazette* Looking at Women and the Family', *Women in Eastern Europe,* No. 2 June, pp.9-13.

Holt, Alix, ed. and trans. (1977) Kollontai, Alexandra, *Selected Writings* (London, Allison & Busby).

Holter, Harriet (1970) *Sex Roles and Social Structure* (Oslo, Universitet Forlaget).

Hough, Jerry F. (1976) 'Party Saturation in the Soviet Union', in Paul Cocks, Robert V. Daniels and Nancy Whittier Heer, *The Dynamics of Soviet Politics* (Cambridge, Mass., Harvard University Press).

Hough, Jerry F. ed. (1977) *The Soviet Union and Social Science* (Cambridge Mass., Harvard University Press).

Hough, Jerry F. (1978) 'Women and Women's Issues in Soviet Policy Debates', in D. Atkinson *et al., Women in Russia* (Sussex, Harvester Press), pp.355-75.
Hough, Jerry F. (1979) and Fainsod, Merle, *How the Soviet Union is Governed* (Cambridge, Mass., Harvard University Press).
Husky, Eugene (1982) 'The Limits to Institutional Autonomy in the Soviet Union: The Case of the Advokatura', *Soviet Studies*, Vol. XXXIV, No. 2, pp.200-27.

Jacoby, Susan (1972) *The Friendship Barrier. Ten Russian Encounters* (London, Bodley Head).
Jancar, Barbara Wolfe (1974) 'Women in Soviet Politics', in Henry Morton and Rudolf Tokes eds., *Soviet Politics and Society in the 1970s* (New York, Free Press), pp.118-60.
Jancar, Barbara Wolfe (1977) 'Women and Elite Recruitment into the Central Committees of Bulgaria, Czechoslovakia and Poland'. Paper presented to *Midwestern Political Science Association* (23 April).
Jancar, Barbara Wolfe (1978) *Women Under Communism* (Baltimore and London, Johns Hopkins University Press).
Jaquette, Jane S. ed. (1974) *Women in Politics* (New York, John Wiley & sons).
Johnson, Chalmers, ed. (1973) *Change in Communist Systems* (Stanford California, Stanford University Press).
Juviler, Peter (1976) *Revolutionary Law and Order: Politics and Social Change in the USSR* (London, The Free Press).

Karnig, Albert K. and Walter, Oliver B. (1976) 'Election of Women to City Councils', *Social Science Quarterly* Vol. LVI, No. 4, pp.605-13.
Kirkpatrick, Jeane (1974) *Political Woman* (New York, Basic Books).
Krauss, Wilma (1976) 'Political implications of gender roles', *American Political Science Review*, Vol. LXVIII, No. 4, pp.1706-23.
Kuhn, Annette, and Wolpe, Ann Marie, eds. (1978) *Feminism and Materialism* (London, Routledge & Kegan Paul).

Lane, Christel (1981) *The Rites of Rulers. Ritual in Industrial Society—The Soviet Case* (Cambridge, Cambridge University Press).
Lane, David (1970) *Politics and Society in the USSR* (London, Weidenfeld & Nicholson).
Lane, David (1976) *The Socialist Industrial State: Towards a*

Political Sociology of State Socialism (London, Allen & Unwin).
Lane, David (1977) 'Marxist Class Conflict. Analysis of State Socialist Society', in R. Scase ed., *Industrial Society: Class, Cleavage and Control* (London, Allen & Unwin).
Lapidus, Gail Warshifsky (1976) 'Political Mobilization, Participation and Leadership: Women in Soviet Politics', *Comparative Politics*, No. 8 (Oct.), pp.90-118.
Lapidus, Gail Warshofsky (1978) *Women in Soviet Society* (Berkeley University of California Press).
Lapidus, Gail Warshofsky, ed. (1982) *Women, Work and Family in the Soviet Union* (New York, M. E. Sharpe).
Lee, Marcia Manning (1976) 'Why Few Women Hold Public Office: Democracy and Sexual Roles', *Political Science Quarterly*, Vol. XCI, No. 2, pp.297-312.
Lennon, Lotte (1970) 'Women in the USSR', *Problems of Communism*, No. 20 (July/Aug.), pp.47-58.
Linden, Carl A. (1966) *Khrushchev and the Soviet Leadership 1957-1964* (Baltimore, Johns Hopkins University Press).
Lipman-Blumen, Jean (1973) 'Role De-Differentiation as a System Response to Crisis', *Sociological Inquiry*, Vol. XLIII (April), pp.105-29.
Lovenduski, Joni (1981) 'The USSR', in Joni Lovenduski and J. Hills, *The Politics of the Second Electorate: Women and Public Participation* (London, Routledge & Kegan Paul).
Lovenduski, Joni, and Hills, Jill, eds. (1981) *The Politics of the Second Electorate: Women and Public Participation* (London, Routledge & Kegan Paul).
Lowenthal, R. (1979) 'Political Legitimacy and Cultural Change in West and East', *Sociological Research*, Vol. LXVI, No. 3.

McAndrew, Maggie (1977) 'The Extent of the Participation of Women in the Soviet Political System' (unpublished M.A. thesis, Essex University).
McAndrew, Maggie (1985) 'Soviet Women's Magazines', in Barbara Holland, ed., *Soviet Sisterhood* (London, Fourth Estate), pp.78-115.
McAndrew, Maggie, and Peers, Jo (1981) 'The New Soviet Woman—Model or Myth?, *London Change*, No. 3, International Reports: Women and Society.
McAuley, Mary (1977) *Politics and the Soviet Union* (Harmondsworth Penguin).
McWilliams, Nancy (1974) 'Contemporary Feminism, Consciousness Raising and Changing Views of the Political', in Jane S. Jaquette ed., *Women in Politics* (New York, John Wiley &

Sons), pp.157-70.
Madison, Bernice (1968), *Social Welfare in the USSR* (Stanford, Califonia, Stanford University Press).
Madison, Bernice, 'Social Services for Women: Problems and Priorities', in Atkinson, D. *et al., Women in Russia* (Sussex, Harvester Press, 1978), pp.307-32.
Maher, Janet E. (1980), 'The Social Composition of Women Deputies in Soviet Elective Politics: A preliminary analysis of official biographies', in Toya Yedlin ed., *Women in Eastern Europe and the Soviet Union* (New York, Praeger), pp.185-211.
Mandel, William, M. (1971), 'Soviet Women and their Self Image', *Science and Society,* No. 35, pp.286-310.
Mandel, William, M. (1975) *Soviet Women* (New York, Anchor Press/Doubleday).
Margolis, Karen (1980), 'The Long and Winding Roads (reflections on 'Beyond the Fragments'), *Feminist Review* No. 5, pp.89-102.
Meyer, Alfred, G. (1978), 'Marxism and the Women's Movement', in D. Atkinson, *et al.*, eds., *Women in Russia* (Sussex, Harvester Press).
Mickiewicz, Ellen (1973), *Handbook of Soviet Social Science Data* (New York, Free Press).
Mickiewicz, Ellen (1979), 'Regional Variation in Female Recruitment and Advancement in the Communist Party of the Soviet Union', *Slavic Review,* Vol. XXXVI, No. 3, pp.441-54.
Middleton, Chris (1974), 'Sexual Inequality and Stratification Theory', in F. Parkin ed., *The Social Analysis of Class Structure* (London, Tavistock Publications).
Millet, Kate (1972), *Sexual Politics* (London, Abacus).
Mitchell, Juliet (1971), 'Women and Equality', in Juliet Mitchell and Ann Oakley eds., *The Rights and Wrongs of Women* (Harmondsworth, Penguin).
Mylnar, Zdenek (1979), 'The Rules of the Game: the Soviet Bloc Today', *Political Quarterly,* Vol. L, pp.403-19.
Morton, Henry Walter and Tokes, Rudolf eds. (1974), *Soviet Politics and Society in the 1970s* (New York, Free Press).
Moses, Joel (1978), 'Women in Political Roles', in D. Atkinson *et al., Women in Russia* (Sussex, Harvester Press).
Mouffe, Chantal ed. (1979), *Gramsci and Marxist theory* (London, Routledge & Kegan Paul).
Mouffe, Chantal (1981), 'Hegemony and the Integral State in Gramsci: Towards a New Concept of Politics' in George Bridges and Rosalind Brunt eds., *Silver Linings: Some Strategies for the Eighties* (London, Lawrence and Wishart).

Nelson, D. (1980), 'Political Participation in Communist Systems', *East European Quarterly*, Vol. XIV, No. 1 (Spring) pp.109-16.
Nove, Alec (1972), *An Economic History of the USSR* (Harmondsworth, Penguin).

Oakley, Ann (1972), *Sex, Gender and Society* (London, Temple Smith).
Oakley, Ann (1974), *Sociology of Housework* (London, Martin Robertson).
Oakley, Ann (1981), *Subject Woman* (Oxford, Martin Robertson).
O'Brien, Mary (1981), *The Politics of Reproduction* (London, Routledge & Kegan Paul).
O'Brien, Mary (1982), 'The Commatization of Women: Patriarchial Fetishism in the Sociology of Education' (Manchester, paper to *British Sociological Association* BSA Conference 'Gender and Society').
Okin, Susan Moller (1980), *Women in Western Political Thought* (London, Virago).
Orum, Anthony (1974), 'Sex, Socialisation and Politics', *American Sociological Review* (April), pp.197-209.

Parming, Tonu (1979), 'Long-term Trends in Family Structure in a Soviet Republic', *Sociology and Social Research*, Vol. LXIII, No. 3 (April), pp.443-66.
Peers, Jo (1985), 'Workers by Hand and Womb: Soviet Women and the Demographic Crisis', in Barbara Holland, ed., *Soviet Sisterhood* (London, Fourth Estate).
Petchesky, R. (1979) 'Marxism-Feminism: transcending the "separate spheres" ', in Z. Eisenstein ed., *Capitalist Patriarchy and the Case for Socialist Feminism* (New York, Monthly Review Press).
Polk, Barbara (1974) 'Male Power and the Women's Movement', *Journal of Applied Behavioural Science*, No. 10, pp.415-31.
Porter, Cathy (1980) *Alexandra Kollontai: a biography* (London, Virago).
Putnam, Robert D. (1976) *The Comparative Study of Political Elites* (New Jersey, Prentice-Hall).

Randall, Vicky (1982) 'State Imperatives and Policies towards Women', paper presented to the conference of, 'Political Studies Association Women's Group' (2 Oct.).
Reed, Evelyn (1977) *Problems of Women's Liberation: A Marxist Approach* (New York, Pathfinder).
Reich, Wilhelm (1972) *The Sexual Revolution. Toward a Self-*

Governing Character Structure (London, Vision).
Rendel, Margherita, ed. (1981) *Women, Power and Political Systems* (London, Croom Helm).
Rosenham, Mollie Schwartz (1978) 'Images of Male and Female in Children's Readers', in D. Atkinson *et al.*, eds., *Women in Russia* (Sussex, Harvester Press).
Rowbotham, Sheila (1970) 'Alexandra Kollantai: Woman's Liberation and Revolutionary Love', *The Spokesman*, Nos. 4 and 5.
Rowbotham, Sheila (1972) *Women, Resistance and Revolution* (Harmondsworth, Penguin).
Rowbotham, Sheila (1973) *Woman's Consciousness Man's World* (Harmondsworth, Penguin).
Rowbotham, Sheila, Segal, Lynne and Wainwright, Hilary (1979) *Beyond the Fragments. Feminism and the Making of Socialism* (London, Islington Community Press).
Rueschemeyer, Marilyn (1977) 'Demands of Work and the Human Quality: an exploratory study of professionals in two socialist countries', *Journal of Comparative Studies*, Vol. VIII, No. 2, pp.243-55.

Sacks, Michael Paul (1976) *Women's Work in Soviet Russia: Continuity in the Midst of Change* (New York, Praeger).
St. George, George (1974) *Our Soviet Sister* (London, Robert Hale).
Salaff, Janet and Merkle, Judith (1970) 'Women and Revolution: the lessons of the Soviet Union and China', *Berkeley Journal of Sociology*, Vol. XV, pp.166-91.
Sapiro, Virginia and Farah, Barbara (1980) 'New Pride and Old Prejudice: Political Ambition and Role Orientations Among Female Partisan Elites', *Women and Politics*, Vol. I, No. 1.
Sayers, Janet (1982) *Biological Politics: Feminist and Anti-Feminist Perspectives* (London, Tavistock).
Schapiro, Leonard (1970) *The Communist Party of the Soviet Union* (London, Methuen).
Schlesinger, Rudolf (1949) *Changing Attitudes in Soviet Russia: The Family in the USSR* (London, Routledge & Kegan Paul).
Schwartz, Janet (1979) 'Women Under Socialism: Role Definitions of Soviet Women', *Social Forces* (Sept.).
Scott, Hilda (1976) *Women and Socialism: Experiences from Eastern Europe* (London, Allison & Busby).
Scott, Hilda, ed. (1978) 'Women in Politics', *International Journal of Sociology*, Vol. VIII, No. 3 (Fall), pp.3-11.
Scott, Hilda (1978) 'Eastern European Women in Theory and Practice', *Women's Studies International Quarterly*, Vol. I,

No. 2, pp.189-99.
Scott, Hilda (1982) *Sweden's Right to be Human. Sex-Role Equality: The Goal and the Reality* (London, Allison & Busby).
Shapiro, Jane (1975) 'The Politicization of Soviet Women: "From Passivity to Protest" ', *Canadian Slavonic Papers*, Vol. XIX (Winter), pp.596-616.
Skilling, H. Gordon (1973) 'Group Conflict and Political Change', Chalmers Johnson ed., in *Change in Communist Systems* (Stanford, California, Stanford University Press).
Skilling, H. Gordon and Griffiths, Franklyn (1971) *Interest Groups in Soviet Politics* (Princeton, N. J., Princeton University Press).
Smith, Jessica (1928) *Women in Soviet Russia* (New York, Viking Press).
Stacey, Margaret and Price, Marion (1980) 'Women and Power', *Feminist Review*, No. 5, pp.33-52.
Stacey, Margaret and Price, Marion (1981) *Women, Power and Politics* (London, Tavistock).
Sternheimer, Stephen, and Lewis, Carol Weiss (1979) *Soviet Urban Management: with comparisons to the United States* (New York, Praeger).
Stewart, Debra W. (1980) 'Institutionalisation of Female Participation at the Local Level', *Women and Politics*, Vol. I, No. 1, pp.37-63.
Stites, Richard (1978) *The Women's Liberation Movement in Russia: Feminism, Nihilism and Bolshevism* (Princeton N. J., Princeton University Press).
Stoll, Clarice S., ed. (1973), *Sexism: Scientific Debates* (Reading Mass., Addison-Wesley).
Summy, Gaye (1973), 'Theory and Praxis of Sexism in the Soviet Union', *Refractory Girl*, No. 4 (Spring), pp.5-10.

Taubman, William (1973) *Governing Soviet Cities: Bureaucratic Politics and Urban Development in the USSR* (New York, Praeger).

da Veiga-Pinto, Françoise (1976) 'Women and Decision Making: a Social Policy Priority'. A synthesis report. Symposium 17-19 Nov. 1975 in *Labour and Society* (April), pp.3-20.
Volgy, T. and Volgy, S. (1975) 'Women and Politics: Political Correlates of Sex-Role Acceptance', *Social Science Quarterly*, Vol. LV (March), pp.967-74.

Walum, Laurel Richardson (1976) *The Dynamics of Sex and Gender: A sociological perspective* (Chicago, Rand McNally).

White, Stephen (1979) *Political Culture and Soviet Politics* (London, Macmillan).
White, Stephen (1983) 'Political Communication in the USSR: Letters to Party, State and Press', *Political Studies*, Vol. XXXI, No. 1, pp.43-60.
Winship, Janice (1978) 'A Woman's World: Woman—an ideology of femininity', in Women's Studies Group ed. *Women Take Issue* (London, Hutchinson), pp.133-54.
Wolchik, Sharon (1981) 'Eastern Europe', in Joni Lovenduski and Jill Hills eds., *The Politics of the Second Electorate: Women and Public Participation* (London, Routledge & Kegan Paul).
Wolchik, Sharon (1981) 'Politics, Ideology and Equality', in Margherita Rendel ed., *Women, Power and Political Systems* (London, Croom Helm).
Women in Eastern Europe Newsletter No. 2, 1977, No. 5, 1982-3.
Women's Publishing Collective ed. (1978) *Papers on Patriarchy* (London, PDC & Women's Publishing Collective).
Women's Studies Group ed. (1978) *Women Take Issue* (London, Hutchinson).

Yedlin, Toya ed. (1980) *Women in Eastern Europe and the Soviet Union* (New York, Praeger).

Zaretsky, Eli (1976) *Capitalism, The Family and Personal Life* (London, Pluto).

SELECTED PUBLIC DOCUMENTS

Buryatskaya ASSR *Zakony i postanovlenie o zhenskikh sovetakh v aimakov, gorodakh, raionakh, posel'kakh, selakh i ulusakh Buryatskoi ASSR. Postanovleniem Presiduma Verkovnovo Soveta Buryat ASSR 28 Aprel' 1961* (Ulen-ude, 1961).

Congresses CPSU
'Report to the 21st Congress 1959', *Soviet Booklet* No. 47 (London, Soviet Weekly, 1959).
'Report to the 22nd Congress of the Communist Party of the Soviet Union' (delivered by N. S. Khrushchev, First Secretary of the Central Committee, 17 October 1961) *Soviet Booklet* No. 80 (London, Soviet Weekly, 1961).
'Report on the Programme of the Communist Party of the Soviet Union and Reply to Discussion', *Soviet Weekly* No. 81 (London, Soviet Weekly, 1961).

Saikowski, Charlotte and Gruilow, Leo, eds., *Kommunisticheskaya Partiia Sovetskaya Soyuza S'ezd II-oi, Current Soviet Policies, 4. The Documentary Record of the Communist Party of the Soviet Union* (New York, Columbia University Press, 1962).
XXII s'ezd Kommunisticheskol partii Sovetskovo Soyuza: Stenograficheskii otchet (Moscow, Politizdat, 1962).
XXV s'ezd Kommunisticheskoi partii Sovetskovo Soyuza: Stenograficheskii otchet (Moscow, Politizdat, 1976).
Documents and Resolutions. The 26th Congress of the Communist Party of the Soviet Union, Moscow Feb. 23-March 1981 (Moscow, Novosti).
Mikhail Gorbachev, Report to 27th Congress CPSU 25 Feb. 1986, trans. *Soviet News,* 26 Feb. 1986.
Ivanovo obkom 'Povyshat' politicheskuyu i proizvodetsvennuyu aktivnost' zhenshchin'. S plenuma Ivanovskovo obkoma KPSS *Partiinaya Zhizn,* No. 16, 1975 pp.39-45.
Kommunist 1981 Kalendar'—Spravochnik (Moscow, Politicheskie literatury, 1980).
Struker, V. I., ed. *Kommunisticheskaya Partiya Sovetskovo Soyuza* (Moscow, Politizdat, 1973).
Kosachkovsky, V. A., ed. *Kommunisticheskaya Partiya Tadzhikistana v dokymentakh i tsifrakh* (Dushanbe, UFON, 1965).

KPSS: Plenums and resolutions

Turkmenian KP *Pravda* 14 Jan. 1962, trans. CDSP Vol. XIV, No. 2 (1962) p.30.
Turkmenian KP *Pravda* 18 June 1962.
'CPSU Central Committee Resolution on the 6th Anniversary of the Great October Revolution' trans. *Soviet News* (London, Soviet Embassy Press Dept., 15 Feb. 1977).
TsK 24-29 June 1959, 'O rabote partiinykh i Sovetskikh organizatsi i sovetov narodnovo khozyaistva po vypolneniyu reshenii XXI S'ezda KPSS ob uskorenii teknicheskovo progress v promyshlennosti i stroitel 'stve' in *KPSS v resolutsiyakh i resheniyakh s'ezdov konferentsii i plenumov, Tsentral'novo Komiteta,* Stenograficheskie otchet (Moscow, Politizdat, 1959; 1964).
Kommunisticheskaya Partiya Sovetskovo Soyuza, Tsentral'nyi Komitet, 'O zadachakh partiinoi propagandy v sovremennykh uslovyakh', stenograficheskie otchet (Moscow, Politizdat, 1962).
'Povyshat politicheskuyu i proizvodetsvennuyu aktivnost' zhenshchin' s plenuma Ivanovskovo obkoma KPSS, *Partiinaya Zhizn,* No. 16 (1975) pp.39-45.

'O merakh po ysileniyu gosudarstvennoi pomoshchi sem'yam imeyushchim detyam, 'O merakh po dal'neisheny ulichsheniyu sotsial'novo obespecheniya naselaniyakh', *Moskovskyi Komsomolets* (31 March 1981).

Rules of the Communist Party of the Soviet Union (Moscow, Progress, 1977).

Rutyantseva, M., Pergament, A., and Gromova, G. eds., *Spravochnik Zhenshchiny Rabotnitsy* (Moscow, Profizdat, 1963).

Slovar' Geograficheskoi Nazvanii SSSR (Moscow, Izdatel'stvo Nedra, 1968).

Spravochnik Partiinovo Rabotnika, Bogolyubov, K. L. ed. (Moscow, Politizdat, 1957).

Spravochnik Sekretariya Pervichnoi Partiinoi Organizatsii (Moscow, Politizdat, 1960; 1979; 1980).

Tolmachevi, A. and Il'nitskaya, G., *Voprosy Ideologicheskie Raboty Sbornik razhneishikh reshenii KPSS* (1954-61 gody) (Moscow, Politicheskoi Literatury, 1961).

Tsentral'noe statisticheskoe upravlenie pri sovete ministrov

All-Union Population Census, 1979, *Pravda* (22 April 1979) trans. *CDSP* Vol. XXXI, No. 16, pp.1-6.

Additional Census Data for 13 Republics, *CDSP* Vol. XXXI, No. 27 (1979) pp.10-12.

Narodnoe Khozyaistvo, Uzbekistana, godu 1977.

Sel'skoe Khozyaistvo Moldavii: Statisticheskie Sbornik (Moscow, 1975).

The USSR in Figures, 1984. Brief Statistical Handbook (Moscow, 1985).

Valentei, D. I., ed. *Zhenshchiny na robote i doma* (Moscow, Statistika, 1978).

Zhenshchiny i deti v SSSR (Moscow, Statistika, 1969, 1985).

Zhenshchiny v SSSR, iz zhurnala Vestnik Statistika (Moscow, Statistika, 1979; 1980).

'Zhenshchiny v SSSR', *Vestnik Statistiki* organ TSSU, SSSR No. 1 (1986), pp.51-69.

Vetrov, V. D., *Voprosy organizatsionno-partiinoi raboty KPSS sbornik dokymentov* (Moscow, izdatel'stvo Polit-literatura, 1973).

'Vyshe uroven' politicheskoi raboty v massakh' (s plenumov partiinikh komitetov i sobranii partiinovo aktiva) *Partiinaya Zhizn* No. 11 (1959) pp.21-6.

Index

Academics, female, 2, 16, 38-42, 43, 76-7
Active builders of communism, 120
Activists, 72-3, 76-7, 97, 115
  attitudes of, 112
  and consciousness, 117-18
Ad hoc see Zhensovety
Age of women in CC, 33-4
Agitprop, 52, 87
Alcoholism, 99-100
Aminova, R. Kh., 55
Andreevna, N. A., 30
Andropov, Y., 51
Anti-religious activity, 92-3
Attitudes
  of activists, 112
  male, 41
  Soviet, 35-45
Autonomy
  of women, 3, 11-12, 123, 127
  of zhensovety, 57, 69, 75, 78

Babadzhanova, R. N., 81
Belyaeva, A. S., 74, 76, 92, 107, 109, 117
Bialer, S., 16, 39, 50
Biologism, 8-9, 43-5, 125, 129
Biryukova, Alexandra, 1, 13, 25, 31, 33, 34, 38, 71

Blekher, F., 82, 86, 113, 116, 121, 124
Bobosadykova, G. B., 74, 84, 107
Bodul, I. I., 71
Borisova, N. A., 54
Borovikova, Z. I., 31, 130
Boyanova, V. P., 68
Brashnikova, E. F., 70
Brezhnev, L., 37, 42, 51, 92
Busheva, A. I., 105

Career advancement, 7, 22
Central Auditing Commission, 28, 35
Central Committee, 21, 23, 24, 25, 27-35
Central secretariat, 28
Cheidene, V., 39, 40, 41, 51, 76, 77, 81, 85, 103
Cherkashina, V. N., 33, 34
Chermenykh, N. I., 58, 61
Chetwynd, J., 9
Child care, 83-4, 103-6, 115-16, 121, 124
Child guidance, 105-6
Chkhikvadze, V. M., 51, 54
Chuprova, L., 104
Class divisions, 10
Commissions for Work

173

Amongst Women, 56, 58-9, 71, 92
Communist party (CPSU)
  age of women in, 33-4
  hierarchy within, 25
  members in zhensovety, 74-8
  membership of, 22-3, 91-2
  nomenklatura system, 3, 21, 24-5, 27, 35, 42, 44, 127
  and social organisations, 50-2
  vanguard role, 21-3, 45, 123, 127
  women in, 25-35
  and zhensovety, 69-72, 90-2, 121, 127
  see also Theory, Marxist, Soviet
Congresses
  21st Party, 49-50
  22nd Party, 51
  24th Party, 25
  25th Party, 71, 83
  26th Party, 29, 32, 34, 83
  27th Party, 28, 31, 34, 37, 83, 108, 123
  14th Republican, 71
  Women's, 53
Consciousness raising, 8-12, 56-7, 65, 72, 125
  and gender roles, 96-110
  significance of, 3
Council of Ministers, 31
Council of Trade Unions, 31
CPSU *see* Communist Party
Cultural activity, 100-3
Cultural level of women, 41, 44, 53, 101, 122

Danilova, Y. Z., 56
Decision making, 27, 28
Defence, 27

Democracy, 13, 36, 49-51, 54, 77
Dement'eva, R. F., 30, 31, 34
Differentiation policy, 52-3, 55, 58, 60, 77, 123
Dirzhinskaiete, L., 84, 89
Discrimination, 41, 44-5, 127
  see also Sexism
Discussion groups, 89
Dobrodzeene, A., 93, 100, 115, 117
Dudurkaeva, K., 68

Economic activities in zhensovety, 82-6, 120-1
Education of women, 7-8, 39, 41, 87, 107
Efimov, M., 22
Egorova, A., 85
Eliseeva, N. G., 30
Elite in Soviet society, 22
Employment, women in, 6-7
  see also Mobilisation, Workforce
Environment, care of, 98-100
Equal rights, 36
Equality
  definition of, 11
  party commitment to, 128
  political, 21
  right to, 6
  and social organisations, 53
Ershova, N. M., 33, 34

Family, 10-11, 108-9
Female bonding, 124
  see also Sisterhood
Feminism, chapter 1 *passim*
  western, 8, 9, 12, 13, 15-16
Fomina, M., 99-100
Formal/informal politics, 49
Frank, P., 22
Friedgut, T., 51, 128
Furtseva, E. A., 29, 30

Gellert, N. V., 35, 130
Gender awareness, 117-18, 128
Gender roles, 9-12, 14, 39-41, 43-4, 83, 96-110, 122, 125
Golubeva, M. A., 33, 34, 42
Golubeva, V. N., 32-4
Gorbachev, Mikhail, 2, 29, 37, 51, 77, 108, 123
Gorbacheva, Raissa, 13
Goricheva, T., 6
Gromova, M. S., 33, 34
Gurtovnik, M., 60-1, 93, 98, 104, 118

Haavio-Mannila, E., 21
Hansson, C., 56
Harsymiw, B., 21, 26
Harnett, O., 9
Hegemony, 51
  male, 11, 16, 127
Heroine mothers, 103-4, 123
Hill, R. J., 22

Ideological work, 27
Ideology, Soviet, 6, 10, 11, 128
Il'chieva, L., 53
Imamova, V., 84
Independence *see* Zhensovety
Initiative, 72-3, 78, 123-4
Interviews, 16
Ivanova, T. G., 30, 31, 120
Ivashchenko, O., 29, 30

Jancar, B. W., 1, 24, 27, 39, 43, 49, 69, 78, 123

Kadeikan, V. A., 41
Kalinina, T. V., 42
Karpova, E. F., 31, 33
Karryeva, R. P., 59
Khmara, I. G., 30, 31
Kirkpatrick, J., 96
Kol'china, O. P., 29-31

Koldova, V. I., 107
Kollontai, Alexandra, 10, 18
Kondrennikov, A. A., 38, 40
Kotelenetz, A. I., 38, 105
Koval', N. A., 17, 58, 88-9, 91, 97, 101, 102, 109
Krest'yanka, 17
Kruglova, Z. M., 29, 30, 33
Krupskaya, N. K., 43
Krushchev, N., 37, 42, 49-50
Kuriedov, V., 82, 117
Kuznetsova, K. P., 68, 117
Kuznetsova, M. S., 76, 77, 102, 118

Lane, Christel, 51
Lapidus, G., 1, 22, 24, 32, 40, 90, 124
Lectures, political, 88
Lee, Marcia, 14
Legislation, 113-15
Leisure evenings, 101-3
Leisure outings, 114
Lenin, V. I., 10, 41, 55, 106-7
Liden, K., 56
Litvinova, G. I., 37, 41
Lykova, L. P., 29, 30, 31

Makeeva, N., 56
Male attitudes, 41
Male hegemony, 11, 16, 127
  see also Political power
Male roles, 106-8
Maria group, 6
McCauley, Mary, 24
McWilliam, Nancy, 9-10
Melnik, Anna, 68
Merkle, J., 43
Methodology, 15-17
Mickiewicz, Ellen, 24
Mitskevich, A. V., 50
Mobilisation of women, 6-7, 51, 52, 83-6, 94, 120-1, 125
Mollaeva, M., 38, 41

Moses, J., 27, 42, 43
Moskvina, M., 56, 68, 132-5
Mosunova, V., 75
Myatieva, A., 70, 75, 84

Nasriddinova, Y. S., 55, 56, 72
New Communist Woman, 11, 32, 81-94, 106, 120-2
Newspaper reading, 91
Nikolaeva-Tereshkova, Valentina, 10, 31, 33, 42, 56
Nizovtseva, A. L., 35
Nomenklatura system, 3, 21, 34-5, 27, 35, 42, 44, 127
Norbu, T. Ch., 75

Oakley, Ann, 11
Okin, S. M., 11
'Olya', 16, 96, 97-8
Oppression, 9
Oral Journals, 89

Paakhava, Anna, 72
Participation in social organisations, 50-1
  see also Political participation
Party Schools, 39
Paternalism, benevolent, 36, 114
Pay, 7
Peace fund, 122
Pereverzeva, N. V., 33, 34
Pletneva, V. N., 29, 33, 34
Poberei, M. T., 30
Polegeshko, A. P., 54, 60, 68, 97, 99, 100, 107, 108
Polishchuk, S. P., 70
Political mobility, 24-5
  culture, 125, 127
  enlightenment, 91, 120, 122
  mobilisation, 120
  see also Zhensovety political activity
Political participation of women, 8, 12-15, 16, 21
  in CPSU, 25-39
  in 'leading' positions, posts of responsibility, 92
  explanations for low, 39-45
  'high' and 'low', 12-13, 126
  see also Politicisation, Socio-economic activity, Zhensovety political activity
Politburo, 25, 28
Politicisation of women, 81-5, 87-94, 109, 112, 122, 125
  see also Consciousness raising
Politics, community, 126
Positive discrimination, 25
Popova, N. V., 37, 41
Power, political, 8, 10, 12-15, 21, 45, 127
  in the family, 11
  see also Male hegemony
Pressure group, zhensovety as, 112-18
Price, M., 15
Primary party organisations, 25-6
Propaganda party organisations, 25-6
  see also Agitprop
Public order, 98-100
Public/private divisions, 9, 12-13, 126

Rabotnitsa, 16-17
Religion, 41, 53, 92-3
Research, 1-2
Role models, 42-3
Rosenham, M. S., 43
Rotar', A. A., 66, 72, 99, 109
Rowbotham, Sheila, 9, 13
Rusakova, V., 104, 116

Rutyantseva, M., 56

Salaff, J., 43
Sapozhnikov, I. N., 52, 60, 90
Scott, Hilda, 11
Sedugin P., 11, 108
Sexism, 9-12, 126
  institutionalised, 21, 44, 127
Shevchenko, V. S., 31, 33, 34
Shitarev, G. I., 59, 70, 74, 77
Sibrayeva, V., 66, 76, 88, 90, 103, 117
Sidirova, T., 16-17, 32, 36, 40, 73, 98
Sisterhood, 117, 124
Slaischeva, N., 39-40
Social organisations, 2, 12, 45, 49-61
  work, 13
Socialist competition, 84
Socio-political activities, 96-100, 122
Source material, 16-17
Soviet Women's Committees, 2, 17, 56
Soviets, women in, 24
Stacey, M., 15
Status of women, 1, 7-8, 27, 31, 75, 86, 113, 123
  see also Biologism, Equality, Sexism
Stites, R., 56, 82, 113, 116
Stoyankina, A. S., 17, 57-8, 66, 69, 71, 72, 75, 83, 86, 87, 93, 96-7, 102, 103, 105, 113, 118, 137, 138
Strepuhov, M., 70
Subbotniks, 60

Tallya, Ol'ga, 11, 13, 16, 35, 39, 40, 43, 45, 54, 57-8, 59, 66, 67, 71, 72, 74, 77, 81-2, 84, 88, 91-2, 93, 107, 116
Tatarinova, N., 23, 55, 83, 113

Theory
  feminist, 14, 16
  Marxist, 11, 42
  Soviet, 2, 11-12, 14, 42, 121, 125, 128-9
Titarenko, S. L., 10
Tokenism, 43
Trade unions, 56, 76, 84, 104, 114
  women in, 22-3
Traditional values, see Gender roles

Udalaya, R. S., 33, 34

Vanguard role see Communist party
Vartik, V., 105, 106
Vetrov, V. D., 16
Voroshilov, 50

Walum, L. R., 15
Western commentary on USSR, 1-2
Western comparisons with USSR, 38
Wolchik, S., 91
'Woman question', 18
Women
  and birth rate, 128
  their confidence, 6
  and peace, 27, 91
  their political invisibility, 13, 14
  and political power, 35-6, 39-40, 126-9
  in social organisations, 2, 12
  and socialism, 41-2
  status of, 1, 7-8, 27, 31, 75, 86, 113, 123
Work
  part-time, 121
  shorter working day, 121

see also Mobilisation
Workplace, zhensovety in, 112-15, 121

Yatrol'skaya, Ts. A., 51
Yemelyanova, Y. D., 42, 43

Zaitsev, 70
Zaripova, N., 56, 88
Zel'dich, K., 75, 117
Zhenotdel, 37, 52-3, 54-5, 113
Zhensovety, 2-3
   activities of, 66, 96-110, 116, 122, 135-8; aims of, 56-7, 113: characteristics of, 55-7; and children, 103-6, 115-16; contradictions in, 125; and CPSU, 69-72, 75-8, 90-2; criteria for assessing, 15-17; criticisms of, 75-7, 94; data on, 17, 139-46; economic activities, 82-6, 120-1; enlightenment, 97; and the family, 108-9; hierarchical structure, 65-9; as independent organisations, 56, 69-73, 77-8, 123; initiative by activists, 72-3, 78, 123-4; local variations, 66, 74, 81; and male roles, 106-8; membership, 67-9; mobilisation 124, and *see* mobilisation; and New Soviet Woman, 81-94, 120-2; party members in, 74-5, 121; political activity, 87-92; as pressure groups, 112-18; and religion, 92-3; responses to, 54; and social organisations, 50-2; spontaneity of, 57-61, 67, 77, 122-3
Zhvirble, S. Ya., 16, 24, 25-7, 38, 39, 40, 41, 74, 77

ABA-3812

WITHDRAWN
From Bertrand Library

AI